PROGRESSIVE

VISION

T H E   C L E V E L A N D

M U S E U M   O F   A R T

June 10 — July 27, 1986

Organized under the supervision of Andrew T. Chakalis

PROGRESSIVE

VISION *The Planning*

of Downtown Cleveland 1903-1930

By Holly M. Rarick   Introduction by Evan H. Turner

The Cleveland Museum of Art

in cooperation with Indiana University Press

The exhibition and catalogue received support from

The Women's Council of The Cleveland Museum of Art;

Forest City Enterprises, Cleveland; and the Ohio Arts Council.

The Herman R. Marshall Memorial Fund

aided publication of the catalogue.

Editing by Sally W. Goodfellow
Design by Laurence Channing
Composition by Bohme & Blinkmann, Cleveland, Ohio 44115
Printing by Great Lakes Lithograph Co., Cleveland, Ohio 44109
Distributed by Indiana University Press, Bloomington, IN 47405

Cover: Detail of architect's rendering, Federal Reserve Bank of Cleveland, ca. 1920

CONTENTS

The title *Progressive Vision* was chosen for this exhibition because it not only fits the tenor of the early decades of city planning in Cleveland but also applies to the feeling that seems to be sweeping the city during the 1980s.

Innumerable architects, planners, historians, and just-plain-Cleveland-enthusiasts, provided the impetus for this project. Special thanks go to Benjamin S. Hubbell and Wallace Teare, who offered their historical perspectives on the subject of early city planning in Cleveland; and to Hunter Morrison and Edward A. Reich, at the City Planning Commission, who continued the dialogue into the realm of present-day city planning.

Objects and information were forthcoming from almost every public and private institution in the city. I am particularly grateful for the assistance of Kermit Pike, Eric Johannesen, and John Grabowski at the Western Reserve Historical Society; Victoria George at Tower City Archives; Judith Cetina and Franklin Peccarillo at the Cuyahoga County Archives; William Becker and Walter Leedy at Cleveland State University; Joan Sorger, Alice Loranth, and Ann Olszewski at Cleveland Public Library; Karen Martinez at the City Hall Public Administration Library; Richard R. Green at Ress Realty Company; Richard B. Bauscherd and Teresa Sedlock at van Dijk, Johnson & Partners, architects; Monica Martinez at AmeriTrust Company; Burton G. Schutach and Harry Thompson at the Federal Reserve Bank of Cleveland; Gertrude Grivnik at the Huntington Building and Bonnie Kopan at Huntington Bank; Katherine M. Klecan at National City Bank; Marian F. Ratnoff at The Higbee Company; Charles Sternberg at Sand's Brass Door Restaurant & Lounge; Norman E. Rusinow and B.R. Atkinson at The Stouffer Corporation; Janet Opaskar and Steven Sankowski at the Federal Building; Patti Graziano at the Plain Dealer Library; Mark Dodd at Cleveland City Hall; and James M. Sutton at the Cleveland Board of Education. The list could go on and on.

Within the Museum, there are those who also deserve special thanks. Andrew T. Chakalis, head of the Extensions Division of the Department of Education, worked long, hard hours in securing objects and related materials for the exhibition; arranging for countless photographs of buildings and interiors; and assisting with preparation of the catalog and the planning, organization, and installation of the exhibition. His unstinting dedication to all of the tasks at hand commands both my admiration and deep appreciation. Laurence Channing, head of the Publications Department, is responsible for the handsome design of the catalog. Also in that department, Associate Editor Sally W. Goodfellow carried out the work of refining the manuscript with patience and good humor; and Hilah Selleck and Karen Cable assisted with manuscript typing. Nicholas C. Hlobeczy, Museum Photographer, provided numerous prints of photographs with dispatch. Education Department Curator James A. Birch and Associate Curator John E. Schloder were supportive, as were staff members of the Extensions

Division — Ann Boger, Robert Dewey, Patrick Gaunt, and Robert Thurmer — who not only offered encouragement but also helped to install the exhibition. Barbara Wamelink, a member of The Women's Council of The Cleveland Museum of Art, proved a continual source of new information and ideas throughout the planning of the exhibition; and several Women's Council members also offered assistance with installation.

Dr. Evan H. Turner, Director, was at all times the guiding spirit for this exhibition. His thoughts, eloquently expressed in the introduction and post-script of this publication, make the exhibition something more than a presentation of historical documents and emphasize the importance of the current interest in city planning for Cleveland.

H.M.R.

Holly M. Rarick, a degree candidate in the Case Western Reserve University/Cleveland Museum of Art Joint Program in Art History, is a Cleveland Museum of Art Fellow for 1985-86.

The 1980s are a time of exciting prospects, as Cleveland is deeply involved in certain major planning decisions that affect the city's appearance and its life in the future. In fact, it may well prove to be the most interesting time in the history of the city since the turn of the century when, deeply stirred by the flamboyance of Daniel Burnham's design for the World's Columbian Exposition (popularly known as the "White City"), a group of enterprising Clevelanders banded together to bring about the realization of a grand plan for the downtown area between Public Square and the lake. All proudly recognized that the Plan—a great plaza of awesome dimensions around which were placed, in the best Beaux-Arts tradition, various buildings responding to the city's needs—was only the second such plan to be created in the United States, 112 years after L'Enfant had designed Washington, D.C.

Today, as the public and the private sectors of Cleveland join together to find solutions to new urban problems, it seems more important than ever that the community understand the planning goals and the philosophy of those earlier citizens. The subject of this exhibition is the challenge that was before the city at its moment of greatest prosperity. It presents the resulting Group Plan—as well as the remarkable defection from it, Terminal Tower—and the various forces, all too often conflicting ones, that were brought to bear in the realization of this ambitious effort between 1900 and 1930.

First, however, this period of great accomplishment should be seen in a broader context, which is easier in Cleveland than it would be in many American cities, since the history of the city's planning process falls conveniently into forty-year increments:

1820-1860: The precise Euclidian plan, with Public Square as the center of a network of parallel streets, initially projected in 1796 by Moses Cleaveland and his companions, establishes the pattern for Cleveland's development, particularly on the east side of the Cuyahoga River to 55th Street but also on the west side—then a separate entity known as Ohio City—to 45th Street. The city grew rapidly in response to the sudden influx of settlers arriving from New England following the opening of the Erie Canal in 1825 and then the connecting Ohio Canal in 1831.

1860-1900: With the railway system in place and the city established as a port, Cleveland becomes the national center of the iron and steel industry by bringing coal from southern Ohio and West Virginia and iron ore and other metals from deposits in the North. The city's industrial leadership commits all of its energies to the development of a laissez-faire expansion first launched with new mills in the Flats and rapidly spreading beyond. The same philosophy becomes the keynote to the development of the city. With the great influx of immigrants from Europe who came to work in the mills, local enclaves develop southward around the mills on each side of the River; as grander prop-

Figure 1. Margaret Bourke-White, American, 1904-1971. *Terminal Tower.* 1928. Gift of Max and Betty Ratner. CMA 85.76.[106]

erties develop beyond 55th Street on the east side and along Franklin Avenue on the west, the earlier Euclidian order similarly gives way to an informality reflecting the more willful whims of landowners.

1900-1940: The city thrives, its growth continuing to reflect in the neighborhoods the same unplanned growth patterns. However, success and affluence having clearly carried the day, a firm commitment to further the public's well-being emerges, and Cleveland's leadership becomes deeply involved in achieving the City Beautiful. The ensuing realization of downtown order in the first three decades of the century is the focus of this exhibition, although some of the earlier ideas of the period are finally developed during the hard years of the Depression; the most notable example is the Great Lakes Exposition of 1936-37, which proves how effectively the shores of Lake Erie can enrich the lives of the citizens. The new sense of public responsibility is impressively evident as well in the creation, around what is now called "University Circle," of various cultural institutions dedicated to furthering the quality of life for all.

1940-1980: Between 1930 and 1955 significant construction virtually ceases, first because of the Depression and then because of World War II. Thereafter, and much more to the point, the fabric of the city, both physically and socially, is shredded: social unrest is widespread, a general exodus to the suburbs burgeons, and whole areas are destroyed in the interests of progress and efficiency. Nonetheless, planning thrives: first, the General Plan of 1949, a general land-use plan for the entire city, as well as public capital improvements, including an extensive highway and rapid-rail plan for a city no longer dependent upon the usual means of public transportation; then, the 1959 plan, which studied the needs of downtown Cleveland; and finally, in 1960, spurred by the availability of urban renewal funds, the Erieview Plan for redeveloping 163 acres extending from East 6th to East 17th Streets—with Erieview Plaza as the focal point—which is then accomplished only in part by the mid-1960s, albeit with flamboyant results. Clearly, all planning is influenced by the prospect of federal funding.

1980-: This period will be considered in a Postscript following the main text and illustrations.

That such an exhibition should be held at The Cleveland Museum of Art may be a source of surprise to some—and yet, with a little consideration, it seems quite appropriate. Since its beginning, the Museum, itself an outgrowth of the same fine community commitment that brought about the creation of the downtown Group Plan, has responsibly maintained high standards in presenting the visual arts. That same point of view is evident as well in its activities in the community: efforts to encourage distinguished works of art as public monuments have been amply demonstrated, and representatives of the Museum have consistently played active roles as members of the city's Fine Arts Commission.

In turn, the exhibitions associated with the Museum's Education Department have repeatedly displayed an innovative approach in presenting ideas associated with the visual arts. Thus, an exhibition nurturing thoughtful consideration of the appearance of the city seems a valid extension of the Department's goals. It is truly appropriate, then, that the gathering of the material for this exhibition should have been done by the Extensions Division of the Education Department — and the realization of this idea is significantly the achievement of its head, Andrew T. Chakalis. Since its founding, the Extensions Division has mounted exhibitions throughout the city and neighboring communities — in 1985, as many as 525 — so it is fitting that this time it draw upon Cleveland's various civic and corporate resources to examine what has happened in a public area of creativity. And, let it be said, the undertaking has occurred none too soon; many of the drawings and plans that provide the basis of this exhibition were misplaced in archives and lost in upper reaches of great downtown buildings.

To assure widespread awareness of the exhibition's focus, after the large exhibition has closed at the Museum, a smaller version, sufficient to convey the thesis, will be shown in various neighborhood centers on both sides of the Cuyahoga River.

An exhibition that records vividly what can happen with energy and commitment has come about because of a comparable spirit of cooperation from a widely divergent group of people and institutions — a group unified, we have found, in their concern for Cleveland's urban planning in the future. As Cleveland now faces the last two decades of the century, the relevance of the earlier thinking will be suggested in a Postscript following the main text of this catalogue.

Evan H. Turner
Director

Like many other Clevelanders, the staff of the Museum is deeply indebted to Hunter Morrison, Cleveland's director of the City Planning Commission, who frequently offered assistance in clarifying details, such as are in this Introduction, but even more importantly, has nurtured an understanding of the great vision of the city's planning process since the earliest years.

Cleveland was a city in transition during the 1890s, trying to cope with a rapid rise in population and a new identity as a major midwestern center for industry and commerce. In less than 100 years Cleveland had grown from a small, malarial-infested settlement established at the mouth of the Cuyahoga River on Lake Erie to become, in 1890, the tenth largest city in the United States. The urban population of Cleveland steadily increased during the decade as immigrants from all over central and western Europe and even China arrived in a steady flow to work in the factories, which threatened to engulf downtown Cleveland.

Proud of their city as a center of industry, yet unwilling to turn their city over completely to factories and soot, members of local government and the Chamber of Commerce began to look into improving the downtown area, particularly around Public Square. Many of these prominent citizens belonged to the pioneering families from Connecticut who had settled in Cleaveland (the "capital" of the Western Reserve) in the early 1800s, establishing the foundations for the city's initial industrial and commercial successes, which in turn led to the prosperity of the 1890s. In these citizens civic pride mingled with a strong sense of civic responsibility; it was their vision for Cleveland that fostered the planning that would make the city both progressive and impressive as it entered the twentieth century.

Even before 1890 Cleveland had been in need of new, larger, more modern buildings to house the city, state, and federal government offices. Cleveland also badly needed new railroad facilities to deal with the ever-increasing passenger and freight traffic. A brand new depot had been dedicated in 1866 and at that time the *Cleveland Leader* proudly proclaimed "...though Cleveland should increase ten-fold in population, still will its [the new depot] ample accommodations be sufficient."[1] Despite this grandiose prediction, by 1890 Cleveland officials were painfully aware that the 1866 depot was far too small to serve the needs of the growing city. The increase in population and the amount of activity going on in downtown Cleveland during the 1890s exacerbated the already-pressing demands for new government offices and better railway facilities.

Along with a desire for new civic and utilitarian structures many Clevelanders sought more cultural institutions. A city the size of Cleveland surely merited a larger public library, a public auditorium or convention hall, an art museum, an art school, and a music hall. Many of the more well-to-do Clevelanders traveled overseas and came back inspired by the great cities of Europe—Paris, Rome, Florence, Berlin, and Madrid—with monumental buildings; wide avenues; and carefully landscaped gardens, parks, and malls. With all the enthusiasm inherent in a rapidly growing city, Clevelanders hoped to emulate the finer points of these well-known cities.

The true inspiration for Cleveland's city plan was to come from a source somewhat close to home. In 1893, after two and a half years of planning and building, the World's Columbian Exposition, fifteenth and largest of the World's Fairs held during the nineteenth century, opened to the public in Chicago, Illinois. Clevelanders who visited the Exposition were undoubtedly astounded at the wonderful "White City" that had been created on Chicago's lakeshore.

The Exposition's architects and designers, under the supervision of Daniel H. Burnham of Chicago, had for the first time created a world's fair that was, in addition to everything else, a pleasing and orderly architectural ensemble rather than just a jumble of individually designed buildings. Their planning, particularly the design for the central Court of Honor with its monumental Neoclassical structures, was based on principles of Beaux-Arts architecture.

In the late nineteenth century, American architects, including the majority of the architects involved with the Exposition, still reverenced and emulated the academic style of French architecture taught to students from around the world at the Ecole des Beaux-Arts in Paris. The French tradition emphasized order and clarity in architecture as well as the absolute necessity for harmonious planning both in the interior of a structure and with regard to surrounding, landscaped areas. Buildings in the Beaux-Arts style are often Neoclassical in design because Neoclassicism

Figure 2. Court of Honor, World's Columbian Exposition, Chicago, 1893. This harmonious arrangement of Beaux-Arts-style structures around a central mall area was the prototype for Cleveland's 1903 Group Plan. [1a]

was considered historically and ideologically suitable for a monumental public or government edifice.

The harmonious grouping of Exposition buildings significantly influenced architectural style and city planning in the United States, particularly in Cleveland. The arrangement of the buildings in a center court around a large mall and huge basin was impressive and overwhelming to Exposition visitors; indeed, it exemplified an ideal solution for city planning. Clevelanders, including city officials and architects, with thoughts of the many buildings in their own city to be erected in the coming years, left Chicago with a vision of a similar grouping that would grace the Cleveland lakeshore.

In 1894, the year following the Exposition, the Cleveland Architectural Club (CAC) was founded. The Club—composed primarily of junior partners in local architectural firms, draftsmen, and artists who had an interest in architecture—in 1895 sponsored a competition entitled "Grouping of Cleveland's Public Buildings." While the results of this first competition aroused some interest, there was no practical benefit for the city of Cleveland.

One of the judges of this first competition, however, was Professor Charles F. Olney, who was also a member of the Chamber of Commerce and a local gallery owner. His participation as a judge in the competition had stimulated a deep interest in the idea of grouping public buildings. By 1898 he was also a member of the Public Library Board, which was considering erecting a new building, and he had convinced the other members of the Board that Cleveland not only needed a grouping plan but that the new library ought to be part of it.

Late in 1898 the members of the Cleveland Architectural Club decided the time was right for a second competition. This time thirty drawings were submitted; Charles Olney again served as a judge. After the competition a public meeting was held, wherein members of the various building commissions were invited to discuss ideas and plans, and enthusiastic citizens also gave speeches. It was evident by now that the idea of a group plan for Cleveland had been firmly launched into the public arena.

An initial formal step was taken on January 17, 1899, when the Chamber of Commerce officially adopted a resolution, introduced by Charles Olney, appointing a Grouping Plan Committee and a consultative body, composed of appointees from the various building commissions, to study the possibilities for a group plan in Cleveland.[2] Thus, the Chamber of Commerce, strongly supported by a committee of highly influential citizens, set out to convince Clevelanders of the desirability of a plan to group public buildings around a central mall. In doing so, they moved Cleveland into the forefront of United States cities practicing city planning.

The special Committee spent the year 1899 trying to raise local interest: efforts included two public addresses and a series of public meetings at which impassioned speeches were given and sites for the grouping were proposed.[3]

One enthusiastic resident, Herbert B. Briggs, wrote of Cleveland and the plan:

How would she [Cleveland] *be known if she were to so plan her coming public buildings as to present to the traveler a reality, in imperishable material, of the past Court of Honor at the World's Fair. She would be known as the only city in the United States, having such an opportunity to grasp its import, to so wisely read the signs of the times, to see the necessity of solving the problem in no other way to meet the progress of the world.*[4]

Beginning the new year and the new decade right, the Committee presented the results of its year-long study to the Chamber of Commerce on January 2, 1900. Recommendations included the proposal of a site and a specific plan for grouping Cleveland's public buildings along the lakeshore, stretching from Erie Street (E. 9th) to Seneca Street (W. 3rd). The southern boundary for the plan was Lake Street (Lakeside Avenue) and the northern border, Lake View Park, was to be extended by filling in the lake to create a park with recreation grounds, featuring men's and women's bathhouses at opposite ends of the east/west axis.

This particular site offered several advantages. The land for the public buildings adjoined one of the public parks, which would serve as a natural frame for the buildings and would not require additional expenditure for landscaping a park. In addition, the area suggested for the buildings was on the edge of a disreputable district that began just northeast of Public Square — the heart

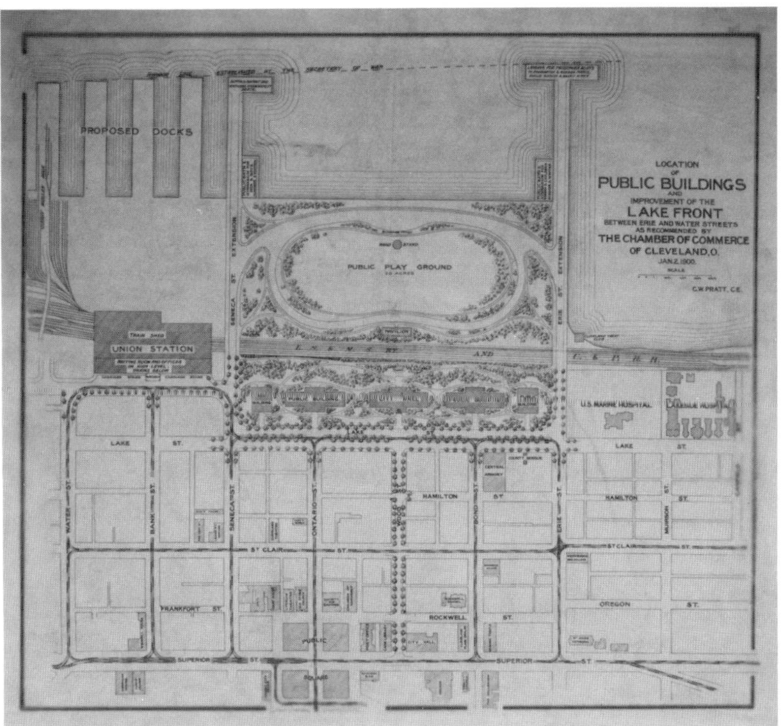

Figure 3. Location of Public Buildings and Improvement of the Lakefront, Cleveland. 1900. Prepared by the Chamber of Commerce, the 1900 Plan grouped Cleveland's public buildings along the lakeshore between Erie (E. 9th) and Seneca (W. 3rd) Streets. The plan features men's and women's bathhouses separated by a twenty-acre playground. [3]

of downtown Cleveland — and extended to the lakefront. In grouping the public buildings at the lakeshore, therefore, the Committee hoped to rid downtown Cleveland of one of its seedier districts and to revitalize the lakefront property.

Committee members also hoped that grouping the buildings along the lakeshore would encourage the owners of the street railways to extend their lines down the wide avenues of Seneca and Erie Streets, thus connecting major business and financial districts with government offices and the recreational areas on the lake.

In response to the 1900 plan, which was enthusiastically received by the Chamber of Commerce, the building commissions for both the Cuyahoga County Court House and Cleveland City Hall determined to build on the lakeshore in the area suggested by the committee. In addition, financiers, architects, engineers, and developers from all over the country came to Cleveland to see the area for themselves in anticipation of a large-scale building campaign.

The grouping of Cleveland's public buildings might well have been realized in the manner suggested by the Chamber of Commerce committee had it not been for the election of Tom L. Johnson as mayor of the city in 1901. This progressive leader, who was either worshipped or severely castigated by his constituents, decided to include the group plan as part of his platform and was one of its staunchest supporters. He recognized its potential and encouraged members of his government to work with the Chamber of Commerce and the local chapter of the Architectural Institute of America to facilitate the creation of the plan.

In 1902 the AIA and Chamber of Commerce presented a bill to the Ohio legislature asking for the creation of a Board of City Planning for Ohio Cities. Though worded in general terms, it was understood by all that the bill applied specifically to Cleveland. The legislature passed the bill and Governor George K. Nash named the following to the three-man commission on June 20, 1902: Daniel H. Burnham, John M. Carrère, and Arnold R. Brunner. The choices were hardly surprising. Burnham, the director of the commission, had been the director of public works for the World's Columbian Exposition and was, at the time of his appointment, involved as a consultant in realizing the 1791 plan of L'Enfant for grouping public buildings around the Mall in Washington, D.C. John M. Carrère was an architect and planner from New York City, who had a record of interest in the Cleveland group plan, having come to Cleveland in 1899 to give one of the public addresses sponsored by the Chamber of Commerce. Carrère's architectural training had been at the Ecole des Beaux-Arts in Paris, and in 1901 he had been responsible for the planning and direction of the Pan-American Exposition in Buffalo. The final member of the Commission, Arnold R. Brunner, was equally qualified and furthermore had the distinction of having already been named as the architect for the U.S.

Post Office, Custom House, and Court House to be built on Superior Avenue at the northeast corner of Public Square.

Thus, by 1902 the city's business and governmental officials had managed to provide themselves and Cleveland with perhaps the three finest architects/city planners in the nation. Having been assigned the task of finding a site and designing a civic center for Cleveland, the three men set up an office in New York City, from which they made consulting trips to Cleveland. In just over a year they produced a plan that captured the attention of architects and city planners all over the world.

Figure 4. Cleveland Chamber of Commerce Building. Completed 1898 (now demolished). Architects: Peabody & Stearns, Boston. Erected on the northeast corner of Public Square, this Neoclassical building was a direct response to the World's Columbian Exposition; caryatids (columns in the form of female figures) adorn the main facade. [2]

1. November 12, 1866, p. 4.

2. Members of the original Grouping Plan Committee of the Chamber of Commerce: William G. Mather, Horace E. Andrews, General George A. Garretson, Rabbi Moses J. Gries, and George W. Kinney. Members of the consulting board, appointees from various building commissions: Board of Education, H.Q. Sargent; Case Library, Samuel E. Williamson; City Hall Commission, Stephen C. Gladwin and Thomas W. Hill; Cuyahoga County Court House Commission, Edward J. Kennedy and W. R. Warner; Library Board, Charles F. Olney and Frank H. Baer; Park Board, Liberty Holden and John H. McBride.

3. The two public addresses were delivered by Harold K. Bush-Brown, a sculptor, and John M. Carrère, an architect and planner who would later be appointed to the Cleveland Group Plan Commission. Both men were from New York.

4. Briggs 1899, pp. 4-5.

In the evening of August 17, 1903, members of the Cleveland City Council gathered to review the plan that Burnham, Brunner, and Carrère had created for grouping Cleveland's public buildings. Mayor Johnson had seen the presentation earlier in the day and according to all accounts neither he nor the members of City Council were disappointed in the proposals made by the Group Plan Commission—the name they used for the appointed architects.

To begin with, the three men had studied the designs and plans of other great civic centers: the Champs Elysées and the Place de la Concorde in Paris, London's Rotten Row, the Royal Palace Belvedere in Vienna, and the Boboli Gardens in Florence, to name a few. Their purpose was not to simply recreate a European civic center; rather, it was to discover the best formula among those that had historically proven successful and satisfying in order to create the ideal civic center to meet Cleveland's particular needs. The magnificent plan they produced, however, rivalled the great European centers both in scale and in format.

Rendered in the Beaux-Arts style, the plan and the presentation drawings depict the proposed buildings as Neoclassical structures surrounded by elaborately designed, landscaped areas. The drawings are large and carefully detailed, and they include proposals for fountains at either end of a mall, as well as aerial views, ground plans, and sections.

Figure 5. European sites that influenced various aspects of Cleveland's Group Plan of 1903. Clockwise from top left: Tuilleries Gardens, Paris (an example of formal gardening lined with formal domestic architecture); Champs Elysées, Paris (city avenue with roadways separated by rows of trees); Place de la Concorde, Paris (formal mall enclosed by two architecturally similar, monumental structures); Palace of Versailles gardens (showing park, fountain, and extended vista). [13a]

The Commission had chosen an area just northeast of Public Square, stretching from Superior Street to the lakeshore, as the site for the proposed grouping of public buildings. The eastern and western boundaries of the Plan were to be Erie Street (E. 9th) and Seneca Street (W. 3rd). Although they considered other sites downtown, the architects based their final decision on many of the same factors that determined the Chamber of Commerce's choice of a similar site in the 1900 plan. The Grouping Plan would effectively make use of prime downtown and lakeshore property that in 1903 was the home of bars, bordellos, and various unsightly establishments. Furthermore, the Mall would face Lake Erie, the source of Cleveland's livelihood and its most attractive feature.

The Commission's choice was determined in part by the fact that the building commissions for both the Cuyahoga County Court House and the Cleveland City Hall had already decided to build their structures near the lakeshore on the sites suggested in 1900 by the Chamber of Commerce. In addition, the site for Brunner's U.S. Post Office, Custom House, and Court House (Old Federal Building) on the northeast corner of Public Square and Superior provided an ideal terminal edge for the Group Plan. The already-determined sites for these three important government office buildings played a large role in the Commission's final decisions as to the size and scope of the Cleveland Group Plan.

Left: Zwingerhof, Dresden (formal park surrounded by formal architecture) [13b]. Right: Champs Elysées, Paris (treatment of statues, vases, and garden seats) [13a].

The main feature of the Group Plan was a grand mall, 560 feet wide, reaching from Rockwell Street to Lake Street (Lakeside Avenue), with an extension on the north end between the Court House and City Hall. The Commission intended this mall as a focal point for downtown life in Cleveland by providing a gathering place for social and civic celebrations.

In the original, 1900 plan a park, extended by landfill, had been proposed for the lakeshore adjacent to the public buildings. Although the Commission acknowledged the attractiveness of having a park that extended to the lakeshore, they also recognized the difficulties inherent in maintaining such a park because of Cleveland's climatic conditions. In addition, the area proposed for the park was dissected by railroad lines, not the most desirable feature for a city park.

Since the railroad lines were in constant use and therefore could not be moved, and since the city was in need of a new railroad depot, the Commission proposed that the depot be a part of the grouping plan. Envisioning the station as a grand building, the Commission proposed placing it between the Cuyahoga County Court House and Cleveland City Hall so as to make it the focal point for the plan. Visitors entering the city by rail would, in exiting the station, find themselves in the city's civic center — a beautiful, gracious mall enclosed by public buildings that reflected harmony in design and arrangement.

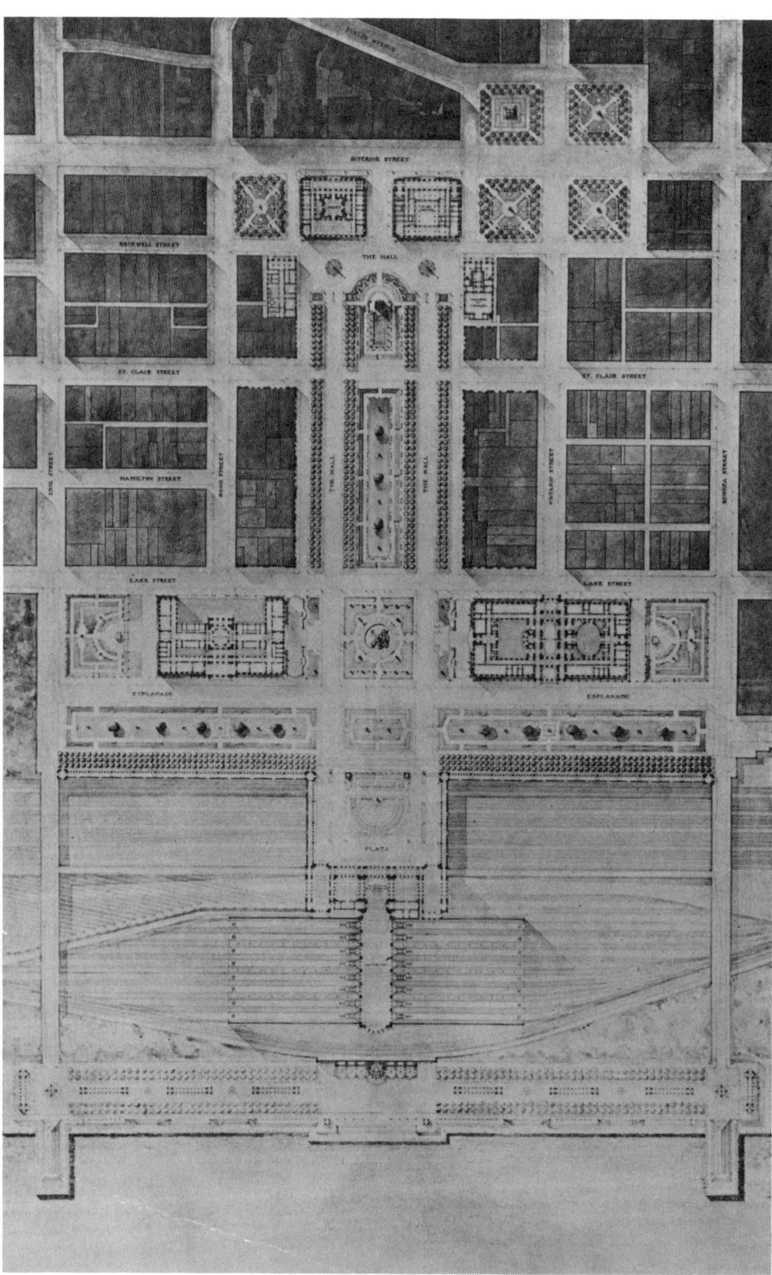

Figure 6. Site plan for Cleveland's Group Plan, 1903, showing Public Square (top right), the Mall, and proposed Union Station and railroad tracks along lakefront (bottom). [4]

Burnham, Brunner, and Carrère had done a thorough job of anticipating and compensating for the problems that might arise in trying to realize their Group Plan. They included in their original presentation a map of the business section of Cleveland indicating the land that in 1903 still needed to be acquired. Of primary concern was the acquisition of land to the east and west of the intended mall so as to ensure conformity of building in the Plan. Their contingency measure was to plant two double rows of trees running the length of the north/south axis, from Rockwell Street to Lake Street, so that if buildings were put up that did not conform to the Plan they would be obscured from view by the trees.

Figure 7. Proposed Union Station on lakefront, flanked by Cuyahoga County Court House (left) and City Hall (right), as viewed from the Mall. [8]

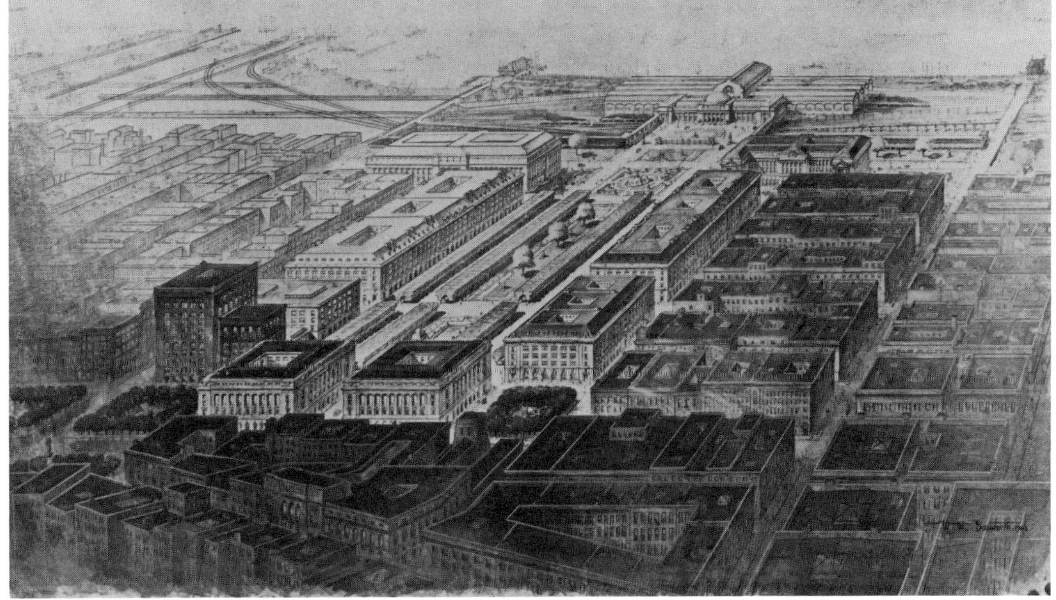

Figure 8. An aerial view of Cleveland's Group Plan, 1903, looking north toward Lake Erie and the proposed Union Station (top). Clockwise from top right, around central mall: Cleveland City Hall, Public Auditorium/Music Hall, Board of Education Building, Cleveland Public Library, Federal Building, Cleveland Chamber of Commerce Building, office buildings, and Cuyahoga County Court House.

In order to hide the smoke of the entering trains from view, the Commission recommended a monumental colonnade with a triple row of trees planted in front of it at the northern boundary of the Mall above the tracks on either side of the station. The Commission had decided that the trees and a colonnade would be more pleasant to look at than a view of the lake obscured by smoke and trains. The Commission also suggested that bridges be built on both Erie (E. 9th) and Seneca (W. 3rd) Streets to cross over the tracks and lead to an esplanade, having bathhouses and walkways, along the lakeshore. Streetcars could approach the lakefront by routes underneath the bridges without disturbing the pedestrians above.

Aside from the Mall, the Commission proposed a park between the railroad station and the Cuyahoga County Court House and City Hall, extending from Erie (E. 9th) to Seneca Street (W. 3rd). Although small parks were planned for the land immediately to the east of City Hall and to the west of the Court House, the Commission acknowledged that this land might need to be put to some other use. The architects also suggested that a certain amount of land be left open just to the east of the library site, since it "would seem most desirable for light, effect, and convenience of the library"[1]; in addition, it would balance the south end of the Group Plan.

At either end of the north/south axis of the Mall the Commission proposed large fountains. For the south end (Rockwell

Figure 9. Fountain proposed for south end of Mall. Group Plan, 1903. [9]

Street) they proposed a triumphal arch with gardens, terraces, formal topiary trees, and a reflecting pool. The walkways flanking the arch were to be lined with Neoclassical sculptures.

For the fountain at the north end of the Mall, between the County Court House and City Hall, their proposal was a trifle more baroque. The detail plan shows only a circular, tiered fountain with four arms that jut out toward the perimeter of the fountain, but the detail elevation shows a remarkable flight of fancy on the part of an unknown designer. The fountain is decorated with dolphins, some bearing *putti* who clasp bows and arrows. On a pedestal in the center, raised above the other figures, is a classically draped maiden who strides forward, trailing a chain

Figure 10. Detail plan for fountain at south end of Mall. Group Plan, 1903.

Figure 11. Detail plan for fountain at north end of Mall. Group Plan, 1903.

Figure 12. Fountain proposed for south end of Mall. Group Plan, 1903.

of flowers. *Putti* dance in a circle around her feet. Water plays over the figures from the mouths of the dolphins and from turtles on rocks at the perimeter of the fountain.

While the Commission may have intended the construction of these particular fountains, they serve primarily as visually appealing aids to illustrate the potential of the proposed Group Plan to Mayor Johnson and the members of the City Council.

Burnham, Brunner, and Carrère recommended that the plans for all the buildings to be included in the Group Plan be derived from "the historic motives of the classic architecture of Rome."[2] As Burnham stated it in his presentation to Mayor Johnson:

The beauty of a great design involving many elements must rest either on picturesqueness, arising from various styles, or on uniformity of style. It needs no argument to prove that in such a composition as this, uniformity of architecture is of first importance, and the highest type of beauty can only be assured by one sort of architecture.[3]

The Commission chose the Roman style of classical architecture primarily because of its order and simplicity, but also because they believed it would have a more enduring influence upon city planning in the future.

They further suggested that the buildings in the Group Plan should be of one material (this was not strictly adhered to, however) and that all the buildings should be of uniform height, width, and mass and, as much as possible, similar design. Burnham spoke for the Commission in justifying these final recommendations:

The jumble of buildings that surround us in our new cities contributes nothing valuable to life; on the contrary, it sadly disturbs our peacefulness and destroys that repose within us which is the true basis of all contentment. Let the public authorities, therefore, set an example of simplicity and uniformity, not necessarily producing monotony, but on the contrary resulting in beautiful designs entirely harmonious with each other.[4]

The architects believed that by establishing a uniform style for the buildings included in the Plan, other city and county buildings erected elsewhere in the city could be similar in style, though not as monumental, and would therefore remind the citizens of the civic center of the city.

The 1903 Plan also included alternative plans for developing the lakefront, if a railroad depot was not constructed. These involved more elaborately designed parks and more landfill. The Commission also suggested, acknowledging that it was not their place to do so, that Clevelanders ought to look to the park land in their city and surrounding areas in order to provide enough parks to meet the needs of a rapidly growing population.

The Group Plan found favor not only with Mayor Johnson (who was to become one of its most vocal advocates) and the City Council but also with the Chamber of Commerce and the citizenry of Cleveland who had developed an interest in the project.[5] The members of the Chamber of Commerce were particularly pleased because the east facade of the Chamber of Commerce Building would face the Mall.

Figure 13. Two alternate
proposals for landscaping
along the lakeshore.
Group Plan, 1903.

The Cleveland Group Plan was heartily endorsed by the American Institute of Architects, who held a convention in Cleveland in November 1903. The plans were exhibited at the World's Fair in St. Louis, where they won a gold medal, and were later exhibited in New York, Chicago, and Toledo. A folio edition of the Group Plan and the text of the original presentation was printed in 1903 and a second edition, with a progress report,

Figure 14. View from Public Square looking toward the Mall site between the Chamber of Commerce Building (left) and the Federal Building (right). Ca. 1910. [16b]

was printed in 1907. In an editorial introduction to the September 1903 issue of the *Inland Architect and News Record* it was said of the Cleveland Plan, "Its lines, though local in purpose, are general in their adaptability to the problem of municipal improvement that confronts every city in the light of modern enterprise and art culture."[6]

National attention was directed to Cleveland in 1903 when it became the first major American city, after Washington, D.C., to propose such an ambitious plan for grouping its public buildings and improving its waterfront. Architects, artists, engineers, and developers came to Cleveland from all over the nation to participate in the realization of the Cleveland Group Plan — the first great city-planning project of the twentieth century.

1. Burnham, Carrère, and Brunner 1903 [1907], p. 3.

2. Ibid.

3. Ibid.

4. Ibid., p. 4.

5. F.E. Cudell, a local Cleveland architect, who had proposed a plan of his own that was rejected by City Council, violently objected to the Group Plan designed by the Commission. He believed that the Mall was too wide for practical use and for aesthetic enjoyment and that the lakeshore was an inappropriate place for government buildings. *See* Bibliography.

6. Unsigned editorial introduction to "The Grouping of Public Buildings at Cleveland," *The Inland Architect and News Record* 42 (September 1903): 13.

I *am much surprised at the splendid work being done by the city of Cleveland and wish to congratulate the city and all parties connected with this progressive work. You are fifty years ahead of most cities. . . .*[1]

To realize a progressive vision requires more than rhetoric from the Chamber of Commerce, elaborate presentation drawings, and civic approval. A successful building program requires time, patience, dedication, and financial resources. Cleveland's progressive vision was realized because a dedicated group of architects, city officials, financiers, and leading citizens were willing to work together at city planning, never losing sight of the ideals behind the original plan.

Burnham, Brunner, and Carrère recognized, however, that certain changes in the original plans might become necessary. And as time would show, they were right. The most significant — and controversial — change was the transference of the site for the proposed Union Station from the north end of the Mall, between the Cuyahoga County Court House and Cleveland City Hall, to the southwest corner of Public Square (1921).

The Best Governed City in the United States

Cleveland was not a city to get caught behind the times in anything. By 1900 six major automobile makers in the city were working to prove that the automobile was going to be more than just a passing fad with the American people. Thus, Cleveland held its first automobile show in 1903 — a most appropriate event for a town that boasted 476 automobiles. In that same year, the year the Group Plan was presented, the corner policeman was made an institution by Police Chief Fred Kohler, who was tired of the eternal complaint: "There's never a policeman around when you need one." On the lighter side, fashion-conscious women in Cleveland kept themselves informed about the latest Paris fashions. And baseball captured both adults' and children's interest: on April 29, 1903, the *Plain Dealer* reported that "Cleveland had gone baseball mad — actually raving mad."[2]

The political leader at this time was Mayor Tom Loftin Johnson, whom the journalist Lincoln Steffens referred to as "the best mayor of the best governed city in the United States."[3] From his election in 1901 until he left office in 1909 Johnson made things happen in Cleveland. He insisted that all "Keep off the Grass" signs be removed from public parks. He held up the land transfer of the site for the future Cleveland Museum of Art until he was assured that there would be days when no admission would be charged. He favored municipally regulated utilities and street railways. He supported women's suffrage. He infuriated citizens by freeing bordello-keepers from prosecution as long as they ran clean institutions and refrained from stealing from the clientele.[4] And he charmed the children in his Euclid Avenue neighborhood by allowing them to use the indoor ice-skating rink he had built behind his home.[5]

Figure 15. Tom L. Johnson, mayor of Cleveland, 1901-1909. Courtesy of The Newspaper Enterprise Association.

Among Johnson's principal beliefs were the rights of the average citizen to have clean streets, adequate police protection, honest merchants, inexpensive streetcar fare and utilities, and honest government officials.

As a progressive mayor, Johnson not only had many friends but also many enemies. Even his enemies, however, favored the Group Plan that he had commissioned during his first term as mayor. A persuasive speaker, he was able to instill his own enthusiasm for the Group Plan in others, thereby establishing a core of citizens and officials dedicated to its completion. He died in 1911, having seen only the first of the Mall buildings completed — the U.S. Post Office, Custom House, and Court House (1910).

Figure 16. View from the west side of Public Square looking east toward site for the Federal Building and the Mall. Ca. 1905. [15]

Johnson's primary contribution was to set the wheels turning for the Group Plan. While he was in office, ground was broken for both the U.S. Post Office (1905) and the Cuyahoga County Court House (1907). The site for City Hall was chosen and plans for the building were drawn up by Cleveland architect J. Milton Dyer (by 1907). And the Public Library Board determined to build their new library on the site of the Old City Hall (1907).

The inevitable red tape, however, began to hamper progress almost immediately. For example: When the cornerstone was laid in 1905 for the U. S. Post Office, expectations were high that the building would be finished in no more than two years; however, delays in federal funding and changes in interior and exterior

Figure 17. Detail of section through the Mall, taken north and south, looking east and showing public buildings in the Group Plan, 1903.

design left the construction crew sadly behind schedule. Thus, the building was not completed until 1910.

Prominent Clevelander William G. Mather said in a prophetic address at the cornerstone ceremony:

It is six years since this idea [the Grouping of Cleveland's public buildings] *began to take root in our minds; its growth has been comparatively slow, but in view of what has thus far been accomplished I am sure no one in the slightest degree regrets this delay. Let us therefore profit by this, and be watchful, so that its complete fulfillment shall not in any way be endangered by any shortsighted policy of haste.*[6]

Frustrations were encountered, particularly during the earliest stages of the Cuyahoga County Court House plan. The Cuyahoga County Board of Commissioners had sponsored a competition for the Court House design. The award-winning design, by the Cleveland architectural firm of Lehman and Schmitt, was an impressive Beaux-Arts design. The local chapter of the AIA immediately protested because the proposed Court House was so large and costly that the other building commissions involved with Group Plan structures could not hope to build something that would be harmonious with the monumental Court House, and thus the uniformity of the intended Group Plan would be destroyed. Consequently, the designs for the Court House were changed, and what exists today is essentially the original design with the final three bays removed from the north and south elevations and two bays removed from the east and west elevations. Instead of a full fourth floor, however, the architects substituted a partial fourth floor.

In April 1906 *The Leader* reported that: (1) changes with regard to the foundation for the Court House had necessitated new plans; (2) these still had to be approved; and (3) members of the County Building Commission expected work to begin on the structure in the spring of 1907.

In the summer and fall of 1906 a controversy raged between the County Commission and certain citizens of Cleveland over whether granite or sandstone should be used for constructing the Court House. Proponents of sandstone argued that it was not only less expensive, but its use would involve an Ohio industry and Ohio workers. Even with the endorsement of sandstone by the United Trades and Labor Council, granite was eventually chosen as the preferred construction material.

Such setbacks during the first years following the approval of the Group Plan could only be expected. After all, has there ever been a successful urban building campaign in which every faction agreed with every decision? Yet the delays with specific buildings did not impede progress in other areas of Group Plan construction and city planning. Among the many important buildings erected during the first decade of the twentieth century were the Williamson Building (1900), Rose Building (1900), Schofield

Building (1902), Citizens Building (1903), Park Building (1904), Union Club (1905), Rockefeller Building (1905), and the Hippodrome Theater (1908).

At about the same time — 1905 — a Chamber of Commerce committee was appointed to investigate the desirability of building a subway in downtown Cleveland. However, the committee, chaired by Worcester R. Warner, reported finally that surface transportation in Cleveland was satisfactory.

In 1906 the City Council adopted a resolution authorizing the appropriation of $1.9 million from an 1862 sinking fund to purchase downtown property owned by the Case School of Applied Science. This land, needed for the Group Plan, included among other parcels the site of the Old City Hall, on Superior Street, which was later to become the site for the Cleveland Public Library, as well as property between Rockwell Street and St. Clair Avenue, which would later become the site for the Board of Education Building.

On December 1, 1906, the City Council approved the new numbering of streets running north and south. Thus, those streets east of Public Square became known consecutively as East 6th, East 9th, and so on, as far eastward as Wickliffe, Ohio; those to the west were similarly numbered, as far westward as North Olmsted, Ohio. Although some citizens regretted the retiring of familiar street names, it was almost immediately recognized that the new system was more efficient and easy to use.

Figure 19. Old City Hall (right), the site chosen for the future Cleveland Public Library. Ca. 1912. The Federal Building is at the left. [53]

By contrast, Cleveland's railroad system in 1906 was anything but efficient, earning Cleveland the unfortunate title "Bottleneck of the Mid-West." The City Council had therefore commissioned Daniel Burnham's architectural firm in Chicago to design Union Station, which the Group Plan had included at the north end of the Mall. With much publicity, the first of many sets of plans was made public in 1906.

Even so, there could be no immediate plans to build the station because the City was embroiled in legal problems with several railroads over a plot of land on the lakeshore between West 9th Street and the Cuyahoga River. Years before, in 1849, the City had "sold" between six and seven acres of that land to the predecessors of the Cleveland, Cincinnati, Chicago & St. Louis; the Lake Shore & Michigan Southern; and the Pennsylvania Railroads. Using landfill techniques, the railroad companies had extended that land to fifty acres. In 1893 the City went to court to recover the land, which they needed for harbor space, claiming that the city had only meant to lease the land to the railroads. Mayor Johnson and the railroads fought one another in the newspapers as well as in the courtrooms.

As if the lawsuit were not enough, the newspapers also published early in 1906 stories of engineers and architects who wanted to build a railroad depot on Public Square, which they considered the heart of the city. Those railroad companies whose trains entered Cleveland from the south greatly favored this idea; for them, Public Square was more convenient than the lakeshore.

Figure 20. Grotesques from the president's office (now destroyed), The Cleveland Trust Company. Above: *Miser Studying His Accounts* [127b]. Right: *Miser Figuring His Profits* [127d]. Far right: *Miser Looking into His Money Box* [127c].

In June 1907 the Erie, the Baltimore & Ohio, and the Wabash Railroads proposed a passenger station for the southwest corner of Public Square, although it was envisioned as more than a passenger station: a twelve- to fourteen-story building could serve both as an office tower and as a station. And the inevitable pollution from smoking trains would be eliminated by electrified subways to the depot. The *Plain Dealer* of June 12, 1907, carried a description of the proposed building, and the article hinted that locally prominent citizens were involved with the project, but no names were mentioned. Less than three years later, however, the Van Sweringen brothers were involved in the creation of a similar project on the same site.

By 1908 the U.S. Post Office was nearly complete and various problems with the Cuyahoga County Court House were all but solved. Mayor Johnson asked Burnham, Brunner, and Carrère to return to Cleveland in October to study the conditions of the city's lakefront so as to develop a comprehensive plan for a large stretch between Edgewater and Gordon Parks. Burnham suggested a lakefront boulevard to run the length of the stretch, a section of which would be elevated over the railroad yards on the West Side.

Simultaneously, a noteworthy event occurred in the nearby burgeoning business and financial center of Cleveland, the area centering on Euclid Avenue and East 9th Street: The Cleveland Trust Company finally completed its new building on the site of what had once been the First Methodist Church. Clearly in harmony with the architectural style of other buildings in the Group Plan, the monumental bank—designed by the New York architectural firm of George B. Post & Sons—boasted a dome similar to that of the Pantheon in Rome. With its Tiffany-style rotunda, the Cleveland Trust Company's great banking hall is the most unusual and beautiful of the many splendid and elaborate banking edifices built in Cleveland during the first three decades of the twentieth century.

Aware that Cleveland was on the brink of a large-scale building campaign, John Carrère encouraged Frank Walker, a young architect from Pittsfield, Massachusetts, to come to Cleveland in 1909. Walker heeded his advice, and went on to lasting fame in Cleveland as a partner in the architectural firm of Walker and Weeks, which he founded in 1911 with Harry Weeks, an old school friend who had settled in Cleveland.

Nineteen hundred and nine saw the first real attempt to use the Mall site as the public gateway area that would reflect the needs of an enthusiastic citizenry. On June 7 the Cleveland Industrial Exposition opened in a temporary building—larger than either Chicago's Coliseum or New York's Madison Square Garden—that had been constructed on the proposed site for City Hall. In twelve days the event drew more than 200,000 visitors.

Meanwhile, local businessmen were setting the stage for events that would occur in the next decade. The Van Sweringen broth-

Figure 21. The new Cleveland Trust Company building at Euclid Avenue and Erie (E. 9th) Street as pictured on a postcard, ca. 1908. [121]

ers acquired four acres of land on the southwest corner of Public Square and had already decided to build their own rapid transit between the residential community they were establishing in the present Shaker Square area, and Public Square. William Rowland Hopkins, who would later serve as Cleveland's first city manager (1924-29), was president of the old Cleveland Underground Transit Company in 1909 when it won approval from the City Council to build a subway system underneath Public Square. That approval carried with it a 75-year franchise, but the project was delayed by the entrance of the United States into World War I and eventually was dropped.

Perhaps the most important event of 1909 was the mayoral election. Mayor Tom L. Johnson, a man who had become a Cleveland institution and was known and respected around the country for his municipal reforms, was defeated by Herman C. Baehr, a West Side brewer whose place in history has all but disappeared. Although Clevelanders had decided to begin the second decade of the twentieth century with new leadership, they would forever be indebted to the great leader who in championing Cleveland's Group Plan had made the city an example to be emulated.

1. Excerpt from a letter received by E. A. Roberts, Secretary of the Cleveland Builder's Exchange, 1907, published in the *Cleveland Plain Dealer*, January 24, 1907.

2. Rose 1950, pp. 633-35.

3. Hines 1974, p. 159.

4. Ibid.

5. Wick 1979, p. 31.

6. May 20, 1905, in Public Square (secured from photo-reproduced collection of quotes dealing with Cleveland's Group Plan in the Public Administration Library, Cleveland City Hall).

I venture to say that this noble conception of a convenient, practical and beautiful civic center, which we call the Group Plan, if carried out as now designed, will redound more to this community's reputation for enlightenment, esprit de corps, and civilization in the highest sense of the word, than any accomplishment of the city since its founding over a hundred years ago.[1]

The second decade of the twentieth century started off well for Cleveland, by now the sixth largest city in the United States. Nineteen hundred and ten was a year of firsts: the first Boy Scout troop was organized, the first taxi-cabs cruised the streets of Cleveland, and the Cleveland Rotary Club was organized. In May Clevelanders watched the skies at night trying to catch a glimpse of Halley's comet and West Siders were surprised when a meteor fell at West 73rd Street and Grace Avenue. On July 4th Minnie the Elephant, waving an American flag with her trunk, led a parade of 10,000 children who had saved their pennies to purchase her for the zoo.[2]

Civic spirit was particularly high in 1910 when the first building in the Group Plan, the U.S. Post Office, Custom House, and Court House—referred to simply as the Federal Building— was finally completed. The official dedication ceremonies for the new building were held in March 1911. Visitors to the building were astounded by the rich use of marble, and they were delighted by a series of murals depicting typical postal deliveries in all parts

Figure 22. West elevation of the U.S. Post Office, Custom House, and Court House (Federal Building). Ca. 1905. [17]

of the world, created by painter Francis D. Millet, an alumnus of the World's Columbian Exposition.

Millet was not the only alumnus of the Columbian Exposition who worked in Cleveland. Since Cleveland was a city with vast financial resources during the first three decades of the twentieth century, both public and private interests retained and paid the best planners, architects, artists, and craftsmen in the country. It was, however, more than money that attracted Burnham, Brunner, and Carrère; sculptors Daniel Chester French and Karl Bitter; and mural painters Sir Francis Brangwyn, Kenyon Cox, Edwin H. Blashfield, Francis Millet, Frederick Crowninshield, and William H. Low to Cleveland. Both the established architects

Figure 23. *The City of Cleveland, Supported by Federal Power, Welcomes the Arts Bearing the Plan for the New Civic Center,* by William H. Low, ca. 1910. Cleveland is enthroned in the center, flanked by Federal Power (left) and the Arts (right). This work was painted on canvas that was then affixed to the wall of the Federal Building; its condition is such that it cannot be removed for display. [21]

and artists who had participated in the World's Columbian Exposition and younger architects and artists trying to establish reputations came to Cleveland because it was a modern city with progressive ideas for city planning.

William H. Low's mural in the Federal Building, entitled *The City of Cleveland, Supported by Federal Power, Welcomes the Arts Bearing the Plan for the New Civic Center*, epitomized the city's enthusiasm and hope for its Group Plan. Cleveland is personified as a dark-haired, fair-skinned, classically draped beauty sitting atop a massive stone throne that rests upon a lakeside pier. Huge pillars spring from either side of the throne with the City of Cleveland seal on the left and the State of Ohio seal on the right. Federal Power rests her sword-bearing arm on Cleveland's knee and holds an oak branch in her other hand. Cleveland welcomes the Arts, who has arrived on a gondola decorated with the Great Seal of the United States. The Arts holds the partially unfurled Plan for the Civic Center in her left hand and behind her stretches Lake Erie, the source of Cleveland's pride.

Low's painting is typical of the many wall decorations created in America's public buildings during the first decades of the twentieth century. His personifications of abstract concepts make Cleveland's welcoming of the Group Plan an episode of monumental proportions.

Figure 24. Newton D. Baker, mayor of Cleveland, 1912-1915. Cleveland Public Library, Photograph Collection.

In 1911 John M. Carrère died and Daniel Burnham resigned from the Group Plan Commission. They were replaced by Frederick Law Olmsted, the famous landscape architect, and Cleveland architect Frank B. Meade; the Commission continued to act in an advisory capacity to the local government. Nineteen hundred and eleven is also remembered as the year in which Sunday baseball was legalized, women whose hat pins extended more than 1/2 inch from the crowns of their hats were liable for a $50 fine, and workmen finally began digging the foundations for Cleveland's new City Hall.[3]

Newton D. Baker became mayor of Cleveland in that same year, but took office early in 1912. Baker was already familiar with Cleveland politics and the city's Group Plan, having served as city solicitor under Tom L. Johnson. During Baker's administration (1911-15), several advances were made toward the completion of the Group Plan.

By 1912 the city had finally completed the acquisition of 104 acres of land that were essential for the realization of the Group Plan: fifty-three acres north of the Lake Shore & Michigan Southern Railway tracks, ten acres of Lakeview Park, and forty-one acres south of Lakeview Park. In addition, the site for the Public Library on Superior Avenue, next to the Federal Building, was officially chosen, more than ten years after the same site had first been proposed.

The much-awaited, much-debated Cuyahoga County Court House opened on January 1, 1912. The plans were the work of

Charles Morris, a designer with the architectural firm of Lehman & Schmitt who had hired Morris at the suggestion of John Carrère. One of the most talked-about features of the new building was the stained-glass window, representing Law and Justice, which was strategically placed to catch the rising sun.

The opening of the Court House was a good omen for the second phase of the Group Plan. Two buildings were now complete, work had begun on a third, 104 acres of land had been acquired, and City Council was prepared to give the deed to the old City Hall property to the Cleveland Public Library as soon as they received the governor's authorization to do so.

The city's commitment to urban planning moved forward significantly in 1913 with the passage of an ordinance to create a City Plan Commission. As its name implies, it was to maintain an overview of the development of business and industrial structures and of the street plans so that as Cleveland increased in geographical size and population, its growth and appearance would be orderly rather than random. The ordinance had no immediate results because the members of the first City Plan Commission were not named until 1915 and monies were not allocated until 1917 for the technical advisors essential for its success.

Public Square was facing changes in 1913: the Illuminating Building was going up adjacent to the northwest quadrant, and the old bandstand on the northeast quadrant was coming down,

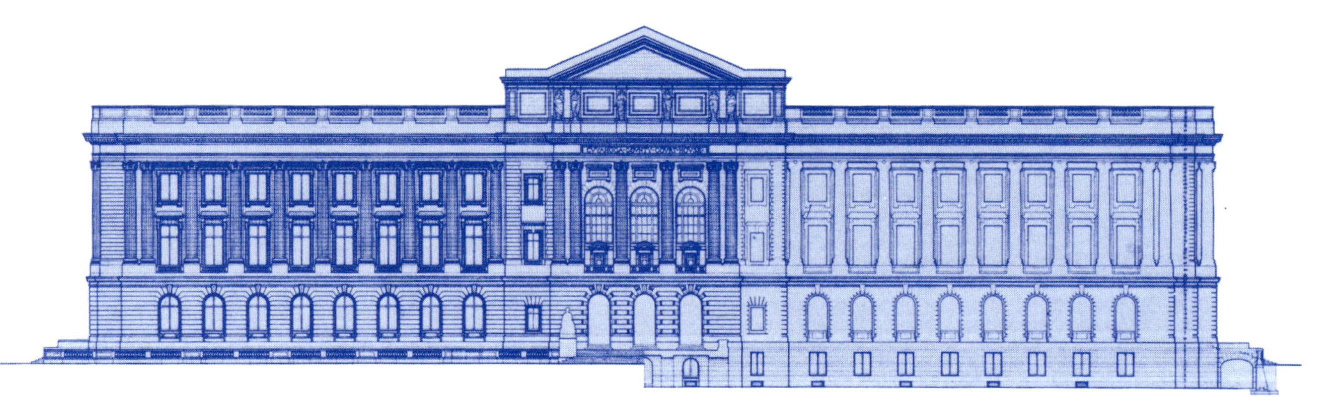

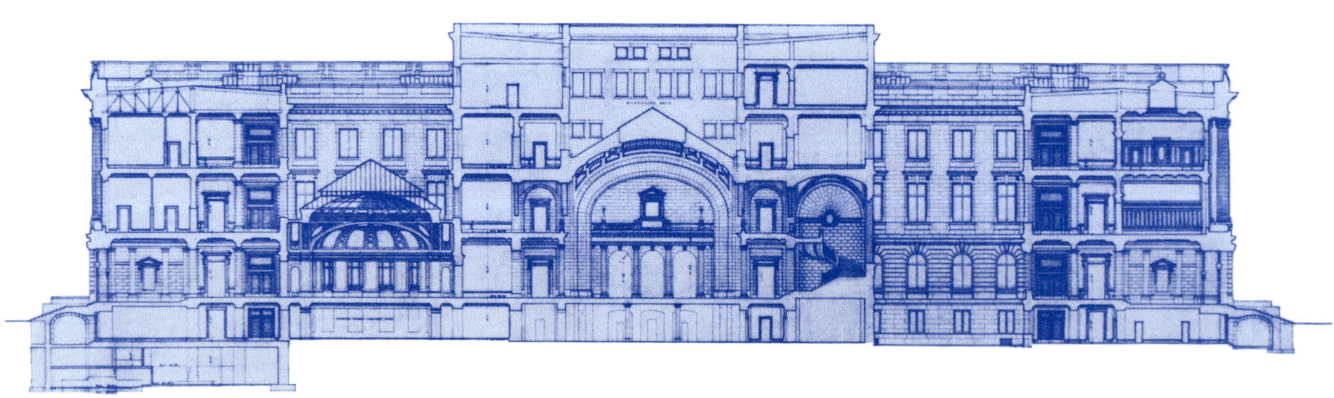

to be replaced eventually with a fountain that was anything but impressive when the water was turned low and sprayed pedestrians when turned up to a normal level.[4] An impressive new building designed by D. H. Burnham and Co., completed in 1912, opened on the southeast side of Public Square; its occupant was The May Company department store.

By 1913 Cleveland was a major center for iron and steel works as well as foundries and machine shops. In addition, however, the city enjoyed national recognition as a center for banking and finance when it was chosen as headquarters for the newly established Fourth Federal Reserve District. The Federal Government had only just passed the Federal Reserve Act in 1913 to regulate currency and to help banks in local communities all across the nation deal with seasonal and emergency needs by assuring that adequate reserves of money would be available via the district branch of the Federal Reserve Bank. The Cleveland office was then (and is still today) responsible for the eighty-eight counties of Ohio, nineteen counties in Pennsylvania, fifty-six counties in Kentucky, and six in West Virginia.

If Cleveland was progressive in its building and city planning, it was also progressive in its approach to giving. In 1913 The Cleveland Federation for Charity and Philanthropy was organized; it allocated funds to Cleveland's welfare agencies, and thus became the prototype for the world's first Community Fund. In 1914 the Welfare Council was established, its purpose being to promote cooperation between public social agencies and private religious, educational, and civic organizations. The Federation and the Welfare Council united in 1917 to become the Welfare Federation of Cleveland.[5]

Another extremely important philanthropic organization formed at this time was The Cleveland Foundation, established in 1914 by Frederick H. Goff, President of The Cleveland Trust Company. The Foundation's stated purpose was to distribute funds "for assisting charitable and educational institutions whether supported by private donations or public taxation; for promoting education and scientific research; for the care of the sick, aged, or helpless; to improve living conditions and to provide recreation for all classes; and for such other charitable purposes as will best make for the mental, moral, and physical improvement of the inhabitants of the City of Cleveland, regardless of race, color, or creed."[6] Indeed, The Cleveland Foundation became a model for similar foundations in other American cities.

Prosperity was the keynote for Cleveland at the mid-decade mark. The Guardian Trust Company had purchased the New England Building on Euclid Avenue and in 1915 the architectural firm of Walker and Weeks began to remodel and enlarge the fourteen-story building. When the building reopened, the customer passed under a facade reminiscent of a temple front and into a grand banking hall of pink marble, decorated with elaborate gilt and bronze fixtures. The president of the company had offices

directly over the entrance with two balconies: one overlooked
Euclid Avenue; the other one, the main banking hall.

Mayor Baker named the first City Plan Commission in 1915.
The list was impressive. Civic and cultural leader Francis F.
Prentiss was named chairman, and other members were Morris
A. Black, Harry M. Farnsworth, William G. Mather, and O.P. Van
Sweringen; added to these influential and prominent citizens
were Cleveland's directors of public safety, public welfare,
finance, utilities, law, and the service director. In 1918 Cleveland
architect Frank Walker and New Yorker R.H. Whitten were
added as technical advisors and Charles E. Conley was named
Plan Engineer.

Figure 27. Preliminary sketches for the south facade of Cleveland City Hall. Ca. 1905. [33b, c, a]

Although Clevelanders did not, of course, realize it at the time, the city was undertaking the last great building campaign before the entrance of the United States into World War I in 1916. Among the many buildings and institutions completed or being built in 1916 were The Cleveland Museum of Art, St. Colman's Catholic Church, Mt. Sinai Hospital, Lakewood Hospital, Lakewood Masonic Temple, St. John's Hospital, and a new wing for Charity Hospital.

In that same year the most important structure in the downtown area was completed: Cleveland City Hall. As the third "corner" of the Group Plan, the building was dedicated on July 4, 1916, with much pomp and circumstance. It would be another six years before a new building—Public Auditorium (1922)—would be added to the plan and another nine years before the Cleveland Public Library (1925) completed the south end of the Plan.

The Library Board held a design competition in 1915-16. Two independent juries were established, one in Cleveland and one in New York. Eight architectural firms were asked to design plans, and of the eight, three were from Cleveland: Walker and Weeks, the firm of Abram Garfield, and Hubbell and Benes, architects of the Art Museum. The latter firm's design was interesting in that it incorporated both a central rotunda and sunken gardens to the east of the building; however, both juries independently selected the Walker and Weeks design. Unfortunately, the United

Figure 28. Pencil rendering of Cleveland Public Library. Ca. 1917. Note the inscription on the entablature, which reads: HOUSE OF LEARNING FOR ALL THE PEOPLE OF THIS PLACE BY GUM! [54]

States entered World War I and the Library project, as was the case with so many other projects throughout America, had to be shelved until such time as men and financial resources were once again available.

Yet another postponed project was a pivotal recommendation made by the so-called Committee of Fifteen. In 1916 a committee of fifteen members representing fifty civic organizations had been created to consider the possibility of Cleveland having a city-manager type of government, in which the city either elected, or the mayor of a city appointed, a city manager, who was responsible for the city's business affairs. Whether it would be advisable for Cleveland was a decision that had to wait until after the War.

Figure 29. Competition designs for Cleveland Public Library, prepared by Hubbell and Benes, Cleveland architects. 1917. Top: Superior Avenue elevation. Bottom: Section through the north-south axis. Their design featured a central rotunda and sunken gardens. [56a, b]

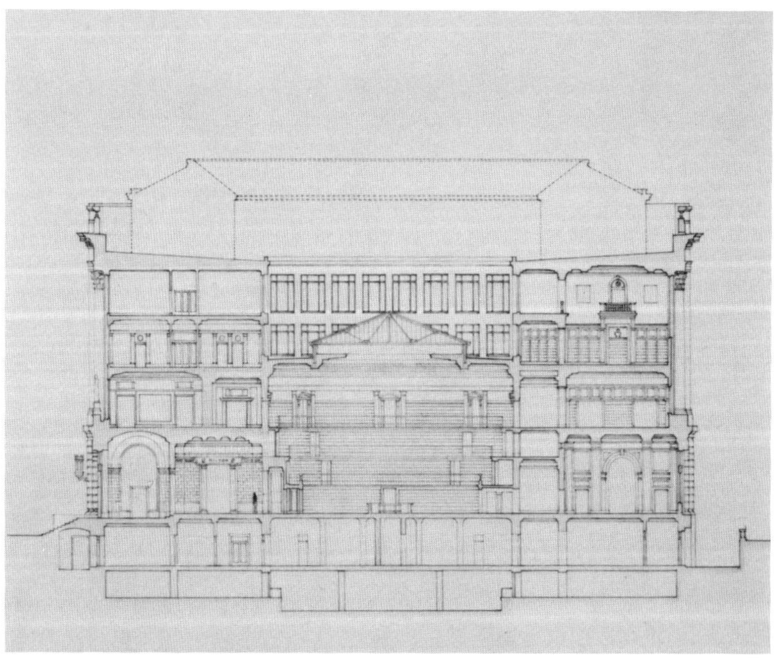

Cleveland was very much involved in a war of its own over the site proposed for the Union Station. Proponents of the Group Plan desperately wanted the terminal at the north end of the Mall, to serve both as the gateway to the city and as the focal point for the entire Group Plan. Unfortunately, the City and the railroads could never quite seem to reconcile their differences; so while they were involved in mediations, the Van Sweringen brothers — Oris and Mantis — were busy at work. We can retrace some of their actions here.

By 1911 the Van Sweringens had become involved in the railroad business and had organized the Cleveland & Youngstown Railroad Company in order to construct a four-track electric rail-

Figure 30. Preliminary sketch of the proposed Union Station at the north end of the Mall. Ca. 1914. [79]

way connecting Cleveland with Youngstown. In 1913 they had made an arrangement with the New York Central to allow that railroad to use half of their C & Y right-of-way into Cleveland, and in 1915 their Cleveland Union Terminal project was legalized by an Ohio law that enabled the electric and the steam railroads to cooperate in building a subway station.

So, by 1915 the Van Sweringens were ready to start building a combined railroad-rapid transit station on Public Square. Their company, the Cleveland Union Terminals Company, had met all the conditions of the city specified by Mayor Newton D. Baker; the City Council ratified the arrangement; and the two brothers began buying up property around the southwest corner of Public Square and along Kingsbury Run, a natural gully running from Shaker Square to Public Square.

Meanwhile, the City had entered into an agreement with the Pennsylvania Railroad and the New York Central Railroad. The City agreed to release its rights to the property "leased" to the railroads in 1849 if the railroads consented to buy a piece of land between West 3rd and East 9th as the site for their new depot, in accordance with the recommendations made by the Group Plan Commission in 1903; consequently, in 1915 Cleveland was faced with the ironic prospect of having two Union Terminals.

By 1915 many people had already questioned the wisdom of having the Union Terminal at the north end of the Group Plan. Certainly it was an aesthetically pleasing arrangement; however, in 1915 it hadn't much else to recommend it, particularly when the Van Sweringen's plan included easy rapid transit access in conjunction with the railroad station, immediate access to Public Square and an office tower, not to mention the large hotel they were going to build right next door to the terminal.

In 1916 the Van Sweringen's project received added support when they purchased the Nickel Plate Railroad from New York Central, and then invited the Baltimore & Ohio, and the Wheeling & Lake Erie Railroads to join the terminal project. All three railroads had declined to be a part of the lakeshore project.

In 1917 plans for both terminals had to be set aside because of the War. By 1918, however, the United States Railroad Administration (USRA) had come into existence, thereby giving the Federal government control of the railroads. Both the lakeshore

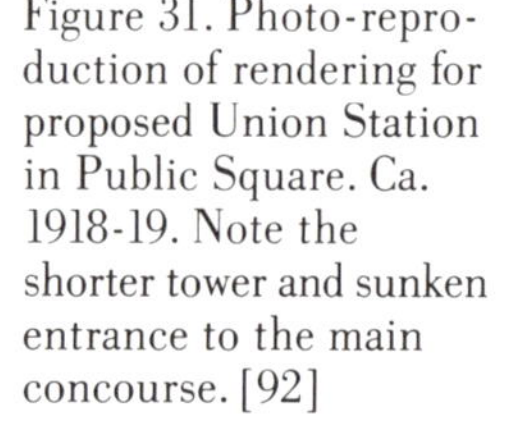

Figure 31. Photo-reproduction of rendering for proposed Union Station in Public Square. Ca. 1918-19. Note the shorter tower and sunken entrance to the main concourse. [92]

project and the Public Square project would require USRA approval for the capital expenditure involved in such a large-scale project. But since both projects could not receive approval, the fight between proponents of the Group Plan and The Cleveland Union Terminals Company was on in earnest. The negotiations of the following years were as complicated as they were ambitious. In 1918 the regional director of USRA, Alfred Smith, an old friend of the Van Sweringen brothers, suggested that they consider making their terminal the Union Terminal for the city of Cleveland. In 1919 Clevelanders voted on the issue and decided in favor of the Union Terminal on Public Square. Passage of the Esch-Cummins Act in July 1920, however, required the Van Sweringens to get the Interstate Commerce Commission's approval for the project as well, adding further complications. In 1921 the ICC held two hearings on the Van Sweringen's request: at the first one, held in Washington, D.C., they denied the request; at a rehearing in August—this time in Cleveland—business, political, social and civic organizations turned out to express their support. The result was that the ICC reversed its earlier decision and finally, in 1923, the first shovel of earth was lifted.

The people who really came out the winners in the battle for the proposed Union Station were the members of the Chicago-based architectural firm of Graham, Burnham, and Company (after 1917: Graham, Anderson, Probst and White), the successor to Daniel H. Burnham's firm. Burnham had been commissioned to do the plans for the lakeshore station, but he had also been approached by the Van Sweringens to design a terminal for the Public Square site. He had rejected their offer, citing a conflict of interest.[7] After Burnham's death in 1912, Ernest R. Graham and the Van Sweringens reached an agreement, and by 1918 the firm had drawn up plans for both projected terminals. Thus, no matter which interest group won the right to build, Graham's firm would be the architects.

After the War

On November 16, 1918, just five days after the Armistice had been signed, Cleveland experienced some temporary "development" of the lakeshore between East 9th and West 9th Streets. Three miles of trenches were dug along the lakeshore and visitors to the nine-day Allied War Exposition got to see soldiers in a make-believe battle on the shores of Lake Erie—complete with tanks and bombers.

Clevelanders could once again pursue the completion of various projects that had been postponed by the War. In December 1918 Hotel Cleveland was completed on the southwest corner of Public Square and Superior; there had been an hotel on that site since 1820. This was the first of the projects by the Van Sweringen brothers on Public Square. They had purchased the land through their Terminal Hotels Company in July 1916 and had begun work almost immediately, only to be halted by the War. The hotel was later joined to the entire Terminal Tower

complex so that guests would not need to leave the building to get to the train station.

In February of 1919 the City Council approved a resolution suggesting that the Library Board begin immediate work on the construction of the new library. The suggestion was welcomed enthusiastically, since the new building would not only complete the south end of the Group Plan but would also aid those citizens who found themselves without work after the War.[8]

The enterprise evident in the planning of the city was to be found as well in a reexamination of its governing procedures. Thus, in the spring of 1919 the Committee of Fifteen resumed its consideration of a city-manager plan of government for Cleveland and by fall gave it their endorsement. Ten of the members suggested that the city manager be elected by the City Council, which itself would be elected by proportional representation on the ballot. The remaining five members of the Committee suggested leaving the government the way it was and having the mayor appoint a business manager for the city. The majority prevailed.

1. William G. Mather, from his address at the ceremony to lay the cornerstone of the Federal Building, May 20, 1905 (secured from photo-reproduced collection of quotes dealing with Cleveland's Group Plan in the Public Administration Library, Cleveland City Hall).

2. Rose 1950, pp. 688-99.

3. Ibid., pp. 699-705.

4. Ibid., p. 720.

5. Ibid., p. 715.

6. Ibid., p. 722.

7. Information received verbally from Dr. Walter Leedy, Cleveland State University.

8. *City Record for 1919* (February 26), p. 199.

hen the transformation is complete Cleveland will not only have remade herself but will have set a magnificent example to other cities. By that time she may have ceased to call herself "Sixth City"—for population changes. But if a hundred other cities follow her with group plans, and whether those plans be of greater magnitude or less, it must never be forgotten that Cleveland had the appreciation and courage to begin the movement in America, not merely on paper but in stone and marble, and that, without regard to population, she therefore has a certain right, to-day, to call herself "First City."[1]

In the first two decades of the century the population had doubled, reaching 796,844 by 1920. Statistics proved that in that same time the city's building activity had doubled as well. Among the city's 125,000 buildings were 14 auditoriums, 23 banks, 76 hotels, 410 churches, 680 agencies of the Public Library, 2,830 grocery stores and butcher shops, and 3,000 saloons. In addition, the city boasted 80 bridges and 2,673 acres of park land.[2]

The 1920s was destined to be a decade of change, experiment, and readjustment for Cleveland. For example, on January 16, 1920, the Prohibition Amendment went into effect and the owners of the city's 3,000 saloons were legally out of business, thus opening up the door to speakeasies.

Harry L. Davis, who had followed Newton D. Baker as mayor, resigned from office on May 1 to run for governor, and William S. Fitzgerald, the City's law director, became mayor — only to be defeated by Fred Kohler the following year. Progress was noted for the Group Plan when the cornerstone was laid for Public Auditorium, which would be completed two years later — a relatively short time compared to preceding buildings in the Group Plan. The year's proudest event, however, had nothing at all to do with city planning: the Cleveland Indians won both the American League pennant and the World Series!

In 1921 the controversy over the site of the Union Station was ended when the Interstate Commerce Commission (ICC) finally gave the Van Sweringen brothers the go-ahead for their Public Square project. Group Plan proponents were naturally disappointed, and some believed the ICC's decision meant the death knell for Cleveland's Group Plan, since the railroad station at the lakeshore would never serve as the grandiose "gateway" for the city of Cleveland. The vast majority of Clevelanders, however, applauded the ICC's decision.

The Van Sweringen's project was more than just an aesthetic showpiece for the city: it was seen as a city within a city, to include offices, stores, restaurants, and even a hotel. But the much-touted importance of the project was that it would provide more jobs for a larger number of people. This was crucial for the city, because in 1921 Cleveland, like the rest of the United States, was suffering from a severe postwar depression. By the end of the year over 125,000 people were unemployed.[3]

Unrest resulting from the depression and unemployment may have been the reason for the surprising outcome of the mayoral election in 1921. Of the candidates who ran for election, the winner was Fred Kohler, an Independent, who had served as police chief under Tom L. Johnson. He was to serve as mayor for only two years, from 1922 until the city-manager experiment was implemented in 1924, but in that time he managed not only to make quite a few enemies but also to change the direction of city planning in Cleveland.

In 1923 *The New York Tribune* wrote, "Mayor Kohler's administration appears to have been largely actuated by the theory that the course to follow is to find out what makes people mad —and then go do a lot of it."[4] One of his first acts as mayor was to reorganize the City Plan Commission and cut the budget from $27,000 to $5,000. He also insisted on painting public property (flagpoles, fire hydrants, traffic signals, crossing lines, tool sheds, and public waiting rooms) yellow and black so as to easily identify items as public property. Unknown citizens cleverly responded to this new measure by painting the turtles in the Public Square fountain yellow and black.

Figure 33. Fred Kohler, mayor of Cleveland, 1922-1924. Courtesy of The Newspaper Enterprise Association.

Kohler insisted that the city be run within the limits of its treasury; in other words, if the money for a project wasn't immediately available from municipal funds, the project never got off the ground. Despite his tightening of the City's belt, the development of certain earlier-approved Group Plan projects continued. The large, impressive Public Auditorium, the fourth building in the Group Plan, opened in 1922. The inscription on its facade read: "A Monument Conceived as a Tribute to the Ideals of Cleveland, Builded by Her Citizens and Dedicated to Social Progress, Industrial Achievements, and Civic Interest."

Construction was finally started on the Cleveland Public Library. The architects, Walker and Weeks, had been chosen by a competition in 1916 and a bond issue for $2 million had been passed to underwrite construction. Unfortunately, the amount was insufficient, so in 1922 the citizens of Cleveland passed a second $2 million bond issue to enable the project's completion.

The Plain Dealer Building at East 6th and Superior, though not actually a part of the Group Plan, was completed by 1922. Architects Hubbell and Benes had designed the structure to harmonize with other Group Plan buildings already completed, and they also were successful in suggesting that the Plain Dealer authorities leave a section of their land open to the west of the building. This resulted in the small park, suggested in the 1903 Group Plan, that was to separate the Public Library and the Plain Dealer Building.

Hubbell and Benes were also involved in a project that was brewing for the north end of the Mall. It seems that a committee of former servicemen appointed by City Council to select a site for a war memorial had chosen the same site as that proposed for Union Station. In a sample plan they had drawn up for the Mall, Hubbell and Benes proposed a Veteran's Building for that

Figure 34. North elevation, Public Auditorium. Ca. 1917. [46b]

same space; public reaction was apathetic, however, so the project was eventually abandoned.

In 1923 the first of many sporting events was held at Public Auditorium. Cleveland's basketball team, the Rosenblums, played the world-champion Celtics. Much to Cleveland's dismay, however, the Rosenblums lost the game by a score of 28 to 24.

The architectural firm of Walker and Weeks remained heavily involved in the neighborhood of Cleveland's Group Plan during 1922 and 1923. Their plans for Cleveland Public Library were finally being realized after seven years of waiting. And in August of 1923 the stunning new Federal Reserve Bank opened and was viewed by the public at a rate of thirty-five people per minute.[5]

Figure 35. West elevation (E. 6th Street), Federal Reserve Bank of Cleveland. 1921. [131b]

The Federal Reserve Bank had been a tremendous undertaking. Initially, twenty-five prominent Clevelanders had been approached for their thoughts on the most appropriate design for the bank. Thereafter, four specialists in bank design worked for thirteen months to define clearly the concept of the bank. At least 1,000 sketches preceded the 1,924 numbered working drawings that were used in construction. Thirty men worked for two years on the plans before the foundations were ever laid. Conceived by Cleveland bankers, designed by Cleveland architects, and built by a Cleveland contractor, the Federal Reserve Bank became a proud statement of the city's fine abilities.

Even as great strides were made in the city's building efforts, Cleveland changed its system of government in 1924 to experiment with a city-manager plan. Clayton C. Townes was elected mayor, the City Council was elected by proportional representation, and the Council in turn elected William R. Hopkins as city manager. According to all accounts, Hopkins was eager and enthusiastic about his position; he served Cleveland from 1924 until 1929. With great interest, the nation watched to see how Cleveland would fare during this experiment with a progressive form of city government, but the experiment lasted only through 1931 when Clevelanders voted it out.

The Group Plan was dealt a severe setback on April 29, 1924. The City Plan Commission had recommended the purchase of a site on the west side of the Mall and the appropriation of funds to construct a building to be used jointly by the City and the County as a courts building. On April 29, Clevelanders voted against both the purchase of the site on the Mall and the erection of the City-County Building. The City-County Building, had it been erected, would have accounted for most of the west side of the Mall and could conceivably have led to the most accurate realization of the 1903 Group Plan.

Within days, however, the gigantic Union Trust Building opened on the northeast corner of Euclid Avenue and East Ninth Street. It soon gained recognition as the second largest office building in the world, and its banking hall (three stories) was the largest in the country. Such grandeur of scale was only appropriate, since the Union Trust Company was, at the time, the fifth largest trust company in the United States.

Cleveland was host to the Republican National Convention in 1924, and delegates spent most of their time in the new Public Auditorium. Frederick B. Edwards, of *The New York Tribune*, wrote in 1923, just after Cleveland had been chosen as the site for the convention:

Certainly beside it [Cleveland's Public Auditorium] *Chicago's Coliseum, in the past the camping ground of many earnestly perspiring Republican conventions, appears hardly more significant than a portable garage for a bungalow's back yard.*[6]

Downtown Cleveland offered twenty-four hotels, with over 6,000 rooms available to convention delegates.

Figure 36. William R. Hopkins, city manager of Cleveland, 1924-1929. Courtesy of The Newspaper Enterprise Association.

Having been the first in the nation (in the 1880s) to install electric lighting for its streets, the city in 1924 acquired a new, improved street-lighting system on Superior Avenue. A less important acquisition that year was the purchase of an excursion boat, the "City of Detroit II," from the Detroit & Cleveland Line. When rebuilt, it was renamed the "Goodtime" and travelled the Cleveland/Cedar Point/Put-in-Bay route.

Meanwhile, William R. Hopkins was busy with big plans for the city: early in 1925 he presented City Council with a recommendation for a large municipal airport. Without an airport, he argued, Cleveland would lose its position as an important U.S. Mail transfer point; furthermore, Hopkins firmly believed that air travel would increase as the century progressed. Thus, on July 1 the new airport (now Cleveland Hopkins International Airport) opened and 100,000 visitors turned out for the dedication, despite the fact that Cleveland's air traffic at the time was limited to eight daily flights — four U.S. Mail trips to the East and four to the West.

Hopkins was also vitally interested in the progress made with the Group Plan. On January 14, 1924, the Cleveland Chamber of Commerce had sent a resolution to the City Council urging that the Council use $1,000,000, which had been made available to the Council through the sale of two serial bonds, to purchase land within the mall.[7] Six months later Hopkins advised City Council that:

The acquisition of property to complete the Mall has been vigorously pressed and agreements reached with all except five owners. The part of the Mall between the Auditorium and East 3rd has been entirely cleared and a sidewalk lain on the east side of East 3rd Street. The area has been sodded from Rockwell Avenue to Lakeside Avenue.[8]

Hopkins's concern for the Group Plan was that even though five buildings had been erected, relatively little had been done towards clearing the mall area and providing for the much-needed landscaping to complement the buildings. A letter dated June 16, 1925, from Olmsted Brothers, the famous architectural landscape firm in Brookline, Massachusetts, made reference to

Hopkins's concern that the City apparently owned no detailed drawings for the Group Plan, and went on to suggest that the landscaping plans were never brought to completion "…partly because of the upsetting effect of war activities, largely because of the controversy over the railroad station site, and partly because of the City's excessive delay in providing funds for the payment

Figure 37. Blueprint for south elevation, Cleveland Public Library. 1919. [57a]

Figure 38. Cleveland industrialist and civic leader William G. Mather (1857-1951). Courtesy of The Newspaper Enterprise Association.

of draftsmen."[9] Subsequently, Hopkins appointed a new Group Plan Committee.

Finally, the new Cleveland Public Library opened its doors to the public in May 1925. A private opening, held on the evening of May 6, was attended by over 3,000 guests who were escorted around the building by 800 library workers called in for the occasion. Quickly gaining national recognition, the Library featured many modern innovations, including a children's room, a newspaper room, and a special section with braille books for the blind.

Clevelanders were not quite as proud of another construction that appeared in 1925. Because the intersection at Euclid Avenue and East Ninth Street was proving to be a trouble spot for traffic, the City erected a traffic tower in the middle of the intersection. Unfortunately, drivers were so interested in looking at the traffic tower that they forgot to pay attention to other traffic and to pedestrians. The tower was hastily removed.

The Cleveland Chamber of Commerce began printing an official monthly journal, *The Clevelander*, in 1926. The second issue included an article by William G. Mather on the development of the Group Plan. Having served as the original chairman for the Chamber of Commerce's 1899 Committee on the Grouping Plan, Mather now wrote:

This is no slight achievement. Imperial city builders have expended larger funds from public treasuries, in shorter periods of time, for

Figure 39. Aerial view of the Cleveland Union Terminals Company project, showing concourse area under construction. Ca. 1928. [102]

Figure 40. Oris P. Van Sweringen (1879-1936). Courtesy of The Newspaper Enterprise Association. [91b]

Figure 41. Mantis J. Van Sweringen (1881-1935). Courtesy of The Newspaper Enterprise Association. [91a]

great and beautiful public works; but a record of more than a million dollars a year for twenty-three years, voted and spent by the citizens of a single community for their own public buildings and for the realization of their own civic ideal, is not easily paralleled.[10]
Some years later, in 1933, Mather received the Cleveland Medal for Public Service for his devotion to city planning and improvements in Cleveland.

Among the 1926 recipients of the Cleveland Medal for Public Service, awarded by the Cleveland Chamber of Commerce, were Oris and Mantis Van Sweringen. The brothers were described as "masters of business, builders of great enterprises, eager participants in every movement for a better Cleveland."[11] Construction of Union Terminal was well under way by 1926, and another two years would see the office tower section (known as Terminal Tower) open for business. By 1927 the steel skeleton for the tower was completed, making the building the tallest in the United States, outside of New York City. Meanwhile, the many evictions due to necessary demolition work for the project created a housing shortage in Cleveland. Hopkins therefore called upon a group of experts to study measures for creating low-rent housing for wage-earners who were being displaced.[12]

The Ohio Bell Telephone Building on Huron Road opened in 1927. Described as a "Temple to Telephony," it was ranked as one of the fifteen finest office buildings in the country by *Nation's Business*, the magazine of the United States Chamber of Commerce.

The Cleveland Industrial Exposition was held in Public Auditorium in 1927. Crowds poured into the Auditorium to see the displays or to listen to transmissions from the Illuminating Company's "Tower of Jewels," which transmitted radio broadcasts via large loudspeakers for pedestrian enjoyment in the mall area west of the Auditorium. The steel-frame tower, standing 221-½ feet tall, was decorated with 20,000 one hundred karat, cut glass Austrian crystals. [13] Attendance for the twenty-three day Exposition was nearly 650,000 people.

City Manager Hopkins also took the opportunity to announce plans for a downtown airfield to be constructed east of the East 9th Street pier. Unfortunately, however, Cleveland was going to have to wait more than twenty years before plans for what is now Burke Lakefront Airport were begun.

By the end of 1927 the members of Hopkins's administration had rallied around the Group Plan, and carefully designed press releases gave the impression that the removal of Union Station to Public Square was the best thing that ever happened. Plans were now being made to extend the Mall straight through to the edge of Lake Erie by cutting a slight grade from the cliff between the Cuyahoga County Court House and City Hall. The serious liability of railroad tracks crossing this area was resolved by the railroad companies agreeing to move some proposed freight tracks to the east, thereby leaving only a few tracks, which could be hidden by landscaping. Simultaneously, the building of a City-County Courts Building on the west side of the Mall was still very much under discussion. [14]

Figure 42. Spectators flocked to see this temporary steel structure resplendent with fountains and 20,000 Austrian cut-glass crystals. Floodlights illuminating the tower cast a combined light of 500 million candlepower. Courtesy of the Newspaper Enterprise Association. [70]

County Courts Building on the west side of the Mall was still very much under discussion.[14]

By 1928 Clevelanders were opening their newspapers and finding headlines like "City's 25-Year Dream of Mall Nears Reality." Enthusiasm for the project was apparent in the finished plans presented for a Board of Education Headquarters Building and by the opening of the Music Hall addition to Public Auditorium, at which time Hopkins said, "This building is dedicated to progress—to the insatiable progress of a great city. . . ." After his speech nearly 10,000 people toured the new building, admiring its Italian Renaissance design.

Plans for the Municipal Stadium to be placed near the north end of the Mall were being drawn up by the architectural firm of Walker and Weeks. Thus, when the city manager was presented with a resolution from the Cleveland branch of the American Institute of Architects urging that the stadium harmonize with other buildings in the Group Plan, Hopkins promised that both the City Plan Commission, which was already making a study of the architecture, and the architects themselves would make a separate study to insure the architectural integrity of the Group Plan.

The Heart of the New Cleveland Trade Empire

Just as the Group Plan was a progressive venture in 1903, the Union Terminal Project, locally referred to as the "City-within-a-City," was a progressive venture for the 1920s. What began as little more than the Van Sweringen brothers' proposal for a rapid transit line from their newly developed Shaker Heights community to Public Square gradually blossomed into plans for a new central business and industrial district, stretching along Ontario Street from Public Square to Orange Avenue, and eventually into plans for what was referred to as the New Cleveland Trade Empire, a railroad empire with Cleveland's Union Terminal as its heart and the Van Sweringen brothers as its rulers.

Oris Van Sweringen envisioned a new type of Group Plan that would aid business and industry, provide a new commercial center for the city, and provide travellers by rail with every possible convenience. At the same time, his project would revitalize Public Square, which had given way to the area around East 9th Street and Euclid Avenue as the city's banking and business center.

The architectural firm of Graham, Anderson, Probst and White created more than twenty schemes for Union Terminal before actual plans were set.[15] The original scheme voted upon by Clevelanders in 1919 had featured a short, stubby tower, and a gigantic entrance under a huge, arched portico supported by monumental columns and pilasters. One of the most interesting aspects of this early design was the treatment of the southwest

Figure 43. Aerial view of the area cleared for construction of Cleveland Union Terminal. Ca. 1923-24. Hotel Cleveland is in the center of the picture. [99]

Figure 44. Rendering of the proposed Union Station, Public Square. In this plan, a round-about replaces the square. [93]

quadrant of Public Square: instead of the level grassy area, the architects provided for a sunken entrance to the shopping concourse in Union Station. Another early scheme showed the tower portion closer to the one that was actually realized in 1928. The tower is taller — though the transition between the lower department store/hotel buildings and the tower itself is too abrupt — making it look as though perched precariously atop the other buildings in the group.

In this scheme, too, Public Square undergoes a magnificent transformation. Rather than a public "square," the designer created a round-about with a huge fountain in the center. However, changing the appearance of Public Square was not an immediate

Figure 45. Public Square elevation, Cleveland Union Terminals Co., Tower Building. 1925, revised 1926. Prepared by Graham, Anderson, Probst & White, Chicago. Courtesy of Tower City Archives, Forest City Enterprises.

concern of the Van Sweringens — clearing the land and building Union Terminal was the primary task at hand. The demolition crew for the project, headed by engineer N. H. Suloff, began the work of razing more than 1,000 buildings in the downtown area. This staggering destruction of the central portion of a large city earned for Suloff the title "The world's greatest wrecker."

Construction had also begun in 1922, and the decision to create a 52-story office tower was probably reached sometime during 1923 — although the public announcement of the change was not made until February 14, 1925.[16] The design for the tower was hardly original, having been inspired by the New York Municipal Building in Manhattan, designed by McKim, Mead and

White and completed in 1911.[17] Indeed, critics have accused the architects of the Terminal Tower of being old-fashioned in their approach, but few can argue that the Van Sweringens' entire plan was not modern in both scope and concept. Intended as a symbol for the city, the Terminal Tower, in the architects' views, was more likely to achieve that status using a design that had already proven successful.

The Tower portion of the Union Terminal complex opened in 1928, and the Chamber of Commerce was quick to move into its fine new quarters in the building and to welcome 4,000 enthusiastic visitors who came to share the event.

On November 19, 1928, the *Plain Dealer* published the projected plans for the "Vans' Super-City," along with a proposed office building adjacent to the Hotel Cleveland and the already-under-construction Medical Arts Building and Builders' Exchange Building. An agreement was reached with the Midland Bank in 1928 to add a third office building, adjacent to the Medical Arts and Builders' Exchange Buildings, to be known as the Midland Bank Building. A brand new, large Main Post Office was also suggested as part of the projected building program. The *Plain Dealer* article concluded:

The dream of the Van Sweringen Brothers, Oris P. and Mantis J., now well on its way to materialization in steel and stone, expresses a profound faith in the future of Cleveland and looks forward to a great metropolitan community.[18]

Figure 46. Illustration from 50th Anniversary Facsimile Edition (1979) of *Cleveland Union Station: A Description of the New Passenger Facilities and Surrounding Improvements.* [96]

The grand official opening for Cleveland's new Union Terminal was held on June 28, 1930, with a formal luncheon for 2,500 guests. Responding to the city's pride and the public's curiosity, the *Plain Dealer* the following day published a thirty-two page supplement describing in great detail the new Union Terminal and the other buildings in the complex. Cleveland could now boast a new, magnificent terminal that was as well-appointed as any other railroad terminal in the entire world.

The Van Sweringens' complex occupied approximately thirty-five acres in downtown Cleveland; it included the three office buildings—Medical Arts, Midland Bank, and Builders' Exchange Buildings; the Hotel Cleveland; the new twelve-story department store (Higbee's) under construction; and the Union Terminal and office tower—all of which were connected by underground streets or passageways. The terminal and office tower alone rested on seventeen acres, and two new streets, 100-foot-wide extensions of Prospect Avenue and Huron Road, were added as part of the project.

Foreseeing yet other needs, the Van Sweringens included in their building campaign the Northern Ohio Food Terminal, located from East 37th to East 40th Streets between Woodland and Orange Avenues. Opening in June 1929, the food terminal was financed by the local produce trade and the Nickel Plate Railroad, which was, of course, owned by the Van Sweringens.

Figure 48. Sketches of light fixtures for Cleveland Union Terminal. Ca. 1926-28. Left: [112c]. Below: [112a].

Figure 47. Main concourse of Cleveland Union Terminal. [117a]

Refrigerator cars full of fresh food, primarily fruits and vegetables, could be switched directly to loading platforms at the food terminal and could then be moved either into storage or directly onto produce trucks.

Most people, then, as now, associated Terminal Tower and Union Station with its most important function as the hub of Cleveland's transportation network. The monumental portico on Public Square — 153 feet long, 36 feet wide, and 47 feet high — was the main entrance to the Union Terminal. Inside the portico was a grand hall with marble floors and a high, vaulted ceiling decorated with ornamental plasterwork. Two main ramps, also marble, led from the portico to the central vestibule. At the end of the vestibule was the main station concourse — 238 feet long, 120 feet wide, and 42-1/2 feet high — with Italian marble walls, fluted pilasters, and an enormous skylight set within an ornamental plaster ceiling. Two additional ramps at either end of the main portico led to the rapid-transit concourses in the northeast and northwest sections of the Terminal. Thirty-one marble staircases connected the concourse areas with either the railroad trains or the rapid-transit trains.

A taxicab stand at the west end of the station was designed to accommodate 125 cars in an area sheltered from Cleveland's unpredictable weather.

Cigar shops, restaurants, cafeterias, a tearoom, private dining rooms, a barber shop, and one of the largest drug stores in the world made up just a small part of the Fred Harvey, Inc., merchandising services included in the station's concourse areas. During lunch hour the various restaurants could accommodate 10,000 diners. The visitor, whether passing through or pausing to spend the night at the famous Hotel Cleveland, found everything he or she wanted within walking distance.

Many Clevelanders came down to the station for no other reason than to admire the beautiful, new bronze and marble appointments. Another popular attraction, though not actually a part of the station, was the observation deck on the forty-second floor of the Terminal Tower, where visitors could see out over the city as well as the lake.

The Van Sweringen brothers had provided a practical, business-oriented group plan for the city of Cleveland that also served to revitalize the heart of Cleveland — Public Square. Certainly the Terminal Tower stands today as a symbol not only of the city but also of the determination of Cleveland's citizens who shared the vision of the Van Sweringen brothers' ambitious building program.

With the Van Sweringen's "Super-City" rising up out of the wreckage of old buildings on Public Square, there was an outburst of renewed enthusiasm for the central downtown area—particularly for the Group Plan. Just as Johnson had made the initial implementation of the Plan an integral part of his campaign for mayor, William R. Hopkins saw the revision and completion of the Group Plan as a responsibility of his administration. Indeed, Hopkins became its spokesman and chief cheerleader.

The late twenties witnessed a succession of important events whose focus was Cleveland's Group Plan. In 1925 the new Public Library opened, and in 1927 thousands of visitors flocked to the recently built Public Auditorium and mall area to view the Industrial Exposition. The following year saw the opening of the splendid Music Hall addition to Public Auditorium. The ·new Board of Education Headquarters Building opened in 1930, and the new Municipal Stadium, in 1932.

Clevelanders were geared for action, and the City was prepared to meet the challenge. With that in mind, Hopkins in 1928 named a new Group Plan Commission: Frank B. Meade, Abram Garfield, and Louis R. Leonard, local architects; Miss Charlotte Rumbold, a member of the Public Arts Commission; Frank R. Walker, architect for three buildings in the Group Plan and consultant for two others; and Albert D. Taylor, a prominent citizen. Their job was to review the original 1903 Group Plan and to revise it to fit Cleveland's future needs, while maintaining the integrity of the original Plan.

A year later they presented a magnificent, revised plan for the Mall and the lakeshore area, which met with nearly unanimous public approval.[19] The chief revision was to open up the north end of the Mall—since the railroad depot had been shifted to Public Square—thereby enlarging and lengthening the original Mall by creating a landscaped plaza that led down to the lakeshore. Instead of a boxed-in Mall, all on one level, Cleveland would have an Upper Mall, perfect for civic functions, and a Lower Mall, developed to take full advantage of the lakeshore. An appealing feature was that from the Cleveland Public Library or the Federal Building at the south end of the Mall, pedestrians could walk down an ever-broadening landscaped area to the lakeshore.

The two main structures on the Lower Mall would be the already-underway Municipal Stadium and a huge exhibition building to the east of it. Along the lakefront itself would be a series of steamship and recreation piers. Thus, the Group Plan would encompass recreation areas, sports events, and expositions to an even greater degree than had been anticipated by the original Plan of 1903.

A tremendous fountain, 200 feet in diameter, was to be placed in the green between City Hall and the Court House. Landscaped terraces would link the Upper Mall with the Lower, and a super-

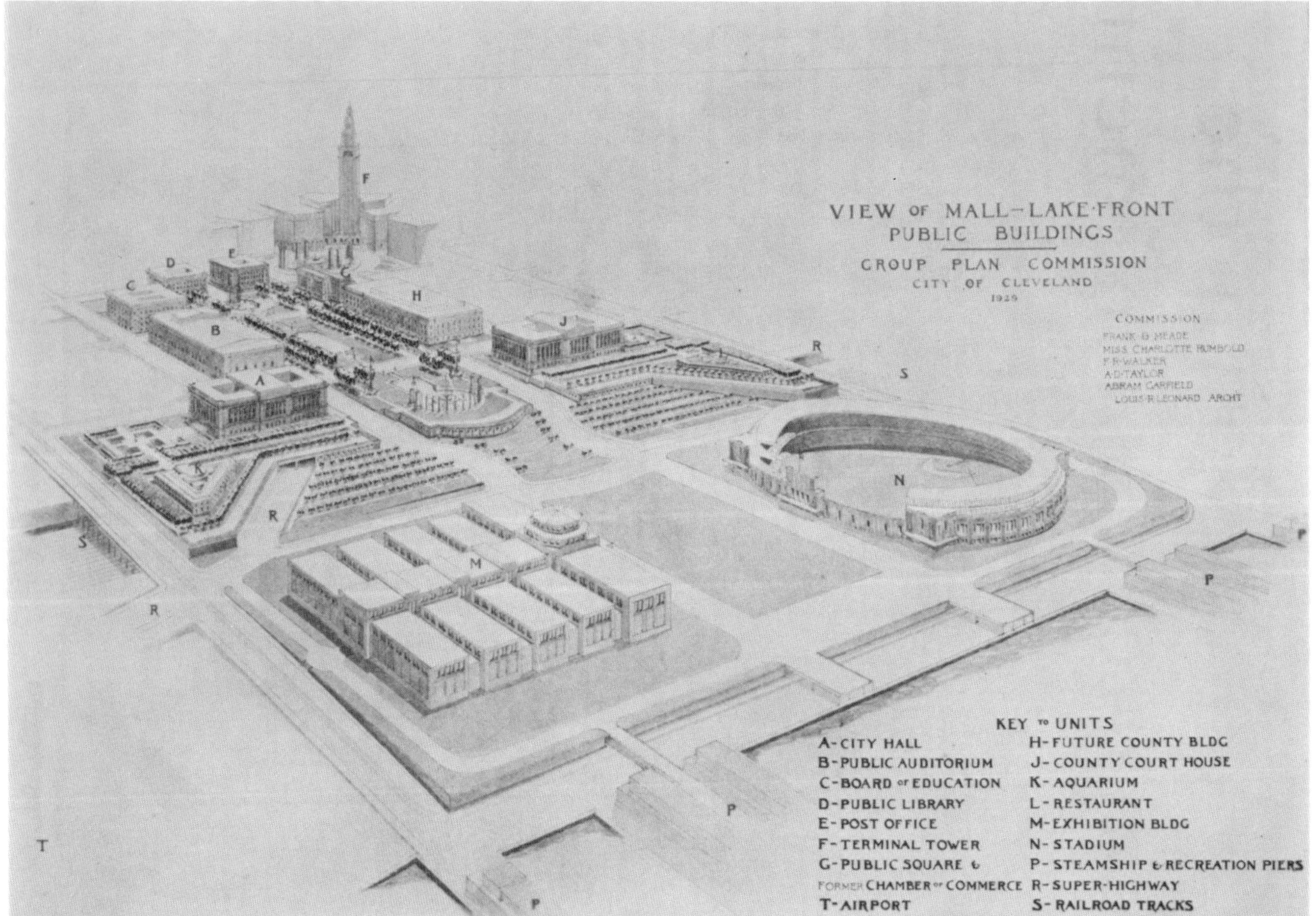

Figure 49. Line drawing of the 1929 Group Plan showing completed public buildings, proposed buildings, and lakefront development. [72a]

highway would run through a tunnel underneath the terraces to connect the east and west sides of the city. An aquarium was proposed for the area just to the northeast of City Hall; and a large restaurant, just to the northwest of the Cuyahoga County Court House. These two structures would balance one another on the terraced portion of the 1929 Plan.

Perhaps the most modern feature of the new Group Plan was the airport proposed for the area just east of the East 9th Street pier. In the 1903 Group Plan, Union Station, along the lakeshore, was to have served as the gateway to the city; with air travel growing in importance, however, the 1929 Group Plan envisioned an airport on the lakeshore as the gateway to Cleveland. Thus, the city would have two gateways, almost on a direct, diagonal line from one another — the new Union Terminal on Public Square for passengers arriving by train, and a lakefront airport for the modern traveller arriving by air.

Members of the 1929 Group Plan Commission, who were all members of the City Plan Commission as well, had taken note of the Van Sweringens' idea of turning Public Square into a roundabout, for they included it in their new plan. In place of the Square would be a central, landscaped plaza with a fountain.

At about the same time, the architectural firm of Walker and Weeks prepared a design for a high-rise office building to complement the south end of the Group Plan. This was not the

first time the architects had suggested a building for the site on the south side of Superior Avenue between, but set back from, the Public Library and the Old Federal Building: with these two buildings placed at two angles of an equilateral triangle, Frank Walker realized that any structure erected at the third angle would serve as the keystone for the south end of the Group Plan.

Since a tall, impressive office tower was the obvious choice for such a site, Walker and Weeks proposed an elegant, streamlined, tiered structure unlike anything else in Cleveland both in size and in scale. Their dream was never realized, however, perhaps because of financial difficulties brought on by the Depression. More than fifty years were to pass before a similar dream was realized with the construction of the Sohio Building (1985).

By 1930 Cleveland had progressed to new, even grander plans for its Mall and lakefront areas. With the completion that year of the Board of Education Headquarters Building, the buildings on three sides of the Mall were a reality and most of the structures on the site for the future Upper Mall area had been torn down. Unfortunately, the city government of Cleveland, like that of most other major cities, had immediately appropriated the newly cleared space for parking areas and temporary structures until such time as the Upper Mall was ready for landscaping.

Five years later, in 1936, it would have been hard for a visitor to Cleveland to imagine that there had ever been decrepit buildings or parking lots on Cleveland's Upper Mall. In 1936 the Great

Figure 50. Renderings for proposed buildings at south end of the Mall. The top one [74] and the one on the right [73] were prepared by Walker and Weeks for the 1903 Group Plan. The bottom one, also prepared by Walker and Weeks, was for the 1929 Group Plan [75].

Lakes Exposition opened and Clevelanders, after more than thirty-three years of patient determination and work, viewed the transformation of a formerly run-down district of the city into a beautifully landscaped center of activity. Hundreds of thousands of people visited the Exposition and marveled at the realization of Cleveland's impressive Group Plan. Though many of the buildings were temporary, the spirit of the people and events that made possible the original 1903 Group Plan was at last captured in the Great Lakes Exposition of 1936. The sons of the earlier generation had realized the progressive vision of their fathers.

1. Street 1914, pp. 61-62.

2. Rose 1950, p. 786

3. Ibid., p. 804.

4. Edwards 1923, p. 5.

5. Rose 1950, p. 820.

6. Edwards 1923, p. 5.

7. *Cleveland City Record*, file no. 62581.

8. *Cleveland City Record*, July 14, 1924, pp. 905-6.

9. Hopkins Papers.

10. Mather 1926.

11. Rose 1950, p. 839.

12. Ibid., p. 851.

13. *The CEICO Motor* (9 August 1927): 6.

14. "The Cleveland Mall Plan," publicity release from the City of Cleveland, Division of Information, December 19, 1927, pp. 1-2.

15. Leedy 1983, p. 15.

16. Ibid.

17. Johannesen 1979, pp. 181-82.

18. *Cleveland Plain Dealer*, November 19, 1928.

19. C. R. 1929.

Figure 51. Aerial view of downtown Cleveland during the Great Lakes Exposition of 1936. Courtesy of The Newspaper Enterprise Association.

Six of the following buildings were constructed, over a twenty-five-year period, as integral parts of the 1903 Group Plan. The remaining five buildings — all banks — are included because their architectural styles are in accord with the style and spirit of the public buildings in the Group Plan, and their construction took place during some of the same years as the public buildings.

The Cleveland Trust Company (1908)
900 Euclid Avenue
George B. Post & Sons, architects

Organized in 1894 and firmly established by 1900, The Cleveland Trust Company had effectively adhered to its policy of "progress with caution." In determining how it was to go forward, however, the Company in 1901 purchased property at the southeast corner of Euclid Avenue and Ninth Street for the erection of a main office building. And by 1903 the trustees voted to consolidate with The Western Reserve Trust Company — a company that had formed in 1900. From 1903 to 1906 the "new" Cleveland Trust Company, in a pioneering move, established fourteen branches in the Greater Cleveland area.

A competition was held for the design of the main building, which presented an unusual challenge to architects, in that the lot at the Euclid-Ninth intersection was a trapezium. Specifications called for a three-story, white granite exterior housing a grand banking hall.

Agreement was reached on a plan that incorporated a rotunda (diam. 61 feet) with an unequal number of bays and a double, glass dome, much like the Pantheon in Rome. With its fluted columns, Corinthian pilasters, bronze doorways and grilles, and marble floors and walls, the interior and exterior architecture echoed the Italian Renaissance style.

Figure 52. Completed in 1908, The Cleveland Trust Company (AmeriTrust Company) building is now surrounded by structures of quite different architectural styles. [119]

Thirteen panels of mural paintings by Francis D. Millet (who only a few years later lost his life in the Titanic disaster) illustrate the development of civilization in the Midwest. Embellishing the main pediment of the building are granite figural sculptures in high relief by Karl Bitter that allegorize the primary sources of wealth: Land and Water, with their concomitant occupations — Industrial Labor, Agriculture, Mining, Commerce, Navigation, and Fishery.

Ground had been broken on December 11, 1905, and the building opened to an admiring public in 1909.

Figure 53. Detail of sculptural figures depicting the *Allegorization of the Main Springs of Wealth*, by Karl Bitter, ca. 1909. [122]

Figure 55. The president's office (now destroyed). [127a]

Figure 56. The main banking hall. Note that near the top Francis Millet's mural paintings are partially visible. [125]

The Federal Building: United States Post Office, Custom House, and Court House (1910)
Northeast side Public Square (bounded by Superior Avenue, East 3rd Street, and Rockwell Avenue)
Arnold W. Brunner, architect

Conceived as occupying an entire block, this building was to contain the Cleveland Post Office, Federal Courts, Custom House, Internal Revenue, Steamboat Inspection, Immigration Service, Pension Bureau, Geologic Survey, Hydrographic Office, and Civil Service Examining Rooms. A five-story granite structure, the building cost $4 million and was the first in the Group Plan to be completed.

Brunner's Neoclassical design was based on a pair of buildings on the Place de la Concorde in Paris (the Group Plan had, in fact, paired the Federal Building with the Cleveland Public Library, to be built later).

On the Superior Avenue side of the building, two freestanding sculptures — entitled *Jurisprudence* and *Commerce* — by Daniel Chester French enhance the end pavilions. The interior contained numerous decorative panels and mural paintings. In particular, the postmaster's office had a total of thirty-five panels, painted by Francis D. Millet, that depict the collection and delivery of mails in countries all over the world. All of these panels have since been removed and are stored in Washington, D.C.

A painting by Kenyon Cox — *Passing Commerce Pays Tribute to the Port of Cleveland* — decorates a wall in a second-floor office, while a large mural entitled *The Common Law*, by H. Siddons Mowbray, is found in the west courtroom on the third floor. The east courtroom, similar in design, has a mural entitled simply *The Law*, painted by Edwin H. Blashfield. In this work, along with allegorized figures, are the figures of men who signify civilizing influences: Moses, Mahomet,

Figure 54. The Tiffany-style dome in the main banking hall. [123a]

Figure 57. A 1986 view of the Federal Building, which now serves as a federal courthouse. [16a]

Justinian, Alexander the Great, Charlemagne, Napoleon, Lord Mansfield, and a bishop and a knight of the time of the Magna Carta.

The court library contains two murals by Frederick Crowninshield that represent *Knowledge* and *Persuasion*. And a judge's chamber includes a mural depicting *The Battle of Lake Erie, September 10, 1813* over a marble mantelpiece; the artist was Rufus Fairchild Zogbaum. Yet another mural, by William H. Low, represents *The City of Cleveland, Supported by Federal Power, Welcomes the Arts Bearing the Plans for the New Civic Center.* Painted on canvas and then affixed to the wall, the work unfortunately cannot be removed for framing and placing elsewhere.

Although the cornerstone was laid in 1905, the building did not open to the public until 1910.

Postscript: A new Post Office was built in 1934 to replace the Federal Building; located on Prospect Avenue, it was the last building in the Terminal Tower group. A new Federal Building was erected at 1240 East 9th Street in 1967.

Figure 58. Free-standing sculptural figures, executed by Daniel Chester French in 1912, represent *Commerce* (left) and *Jurisprudence* (right) [20b, a].

Cuyahoga County Court House (1912)
1 Lakeside Avenue (Lakeside at Ontario)
Lehman & Schmitt, architects

The site for the second building in the Group Plan had been chosen in 1900, and construction began in 1905. The architects' principal designer was Charles Morris, who had received his training at the Ecole des Beaux-Arts. The mid-eighteenth-century Hôtel de Cité in Nancy, France, served as a model for the Court House.

Sculptures decorating the granite facade trace the evolution of the English and American legal systems. Marble statues on the north cornice represent Moses and Gregory the Great, executed by the sculptor Herman Matzen; and the Roman emperor Justinian and the English king Alfred the Great, by Isadore Konti. The south cornice bears six marble figures: Archbishop of Canterbury

Figure 59. Main facade of the Hôtel de Cité, as illustrated in a 1906 publication. [23]

Figure 60. Main facade of the Cuyahoga County Court House. [22]

Stephen Langton and Simon de Montfort, by Herbert Adams; King Edward I and John Hampden, by Daniel Chester French; and John Somers and William Murray, earl of Mansfield, by Karl Bitter. Flanking the main entrance to the building are impressive, seated figures of Thomas Jefferson and Alexander Hamilton, executed in bronze by Karl Bitter. Two other bronzes, executed by Herbert Adams, of Chief Justice John Marshall and Ohio Supreme Court Justice Rufus P. Ranney, flank the north entrance.

The building's grand interior, partly the design of Cleveland architect Charles Schweinfurth, consisted of marble floors and staircases; vaulted spaces; courtrooms in English oak, chestnut, and other woods; skylights (covered during and since World War II); a large, Tiffany-style stained glass window; and paintings, murals, and inscriptions. The stained glass window, designed by Frederick

Figure 61. Interior view of the lobby area. [30]

Wilson and Schweinfurth, depicts Justice with her eyes not covered by a blindfold — as in traditional representations — implying that Justice should see the spirit of the law as well as the letter of the law.

Mural paintings, executed during 1912/13, include *The Constitutional Convention, September 17, 1787* by Violet Oakley of Philadelphia; *King John Signing the Magna Carta at Runnymede* by Sir Frank Brangwyn, R. A., of London; *The Trial of Captain John Smith* and *The Conclave between Pontiac and Rogers' Rangers at the Cuyahoga River, November 1760* by Charles Yardley Turner of New York; *A New England Town Meeting* by Max Bohm; and *Appeal* by Frederick Wilson.

Figure 62. Sculptures flanking the main entrance: *Alexander Hamilton* (left) and *Thomas Jefferson* (right). Both were executed by Karl Bitter, ca. 1909-11. [29c, b]

Figure 63. One of the handsome ornamental bronze gates in the Cuyahoga County Court House. [31]

*New England Building/Guardian Building/
National City Bank Building (1916-17)*
629 Euclid Avenue
Original building: Charles Schweinfurth,
architect
Remodeled building: Walker & Weeks,
architects

The New England Building opened in
1896, but by 1914 it was purchased by
Guardian Trust Company, and the name
was changed to the Guardian Building.
Architects Frank Walker and Harry Weeks
were responsible for an extensive re-
modeling and enlarging plan in 1916-17
that added two floors and 550 rooms to
the structure. Corinthian columns
adorned the new facade of the three lower
stories, and pink marble was utilized for
the majestic banking hall and public
areas inside. Furnishings and decorative
details were elaborate — a pink marble
fountain with bronze falcons; bronze
gates; light fixtures bearing emaciated-lion
shields; and gilt embellishments.

At the close of the bank holiday in 1933,
Guardian was forced to liquidate as a
result of mismanagement. Twelve years
later, in 1945, the building was purchased
by National City Bank. Next door to the
Guardian Building was the National City
Bank Building at Euclid Avenue and
East 6th Street (formerly known as the
Garfield Building before being acquired
by NCB in 1921), so it was only natural
that the two buildings be connected by
their mutual owner. Since 1946 the inter-
connected buildings have been referred
to as National City Bank and the East
6th Building.

Postscript: Walker and Weeks, after
this project, were to eventually design
sixty banks in Ohio.

Figure 64. The grandeur
of these interior views
of National City Bank
reflects the work of
Cleveland architects
Frank Walker and Harry
Weeks in 1916-17.
[128b, c, d]

Cleveland City Hall (1916)
601 Lakeside Avenue (Lakeside at
East 6th Street)
J. Milton Dyer, architect

The 4th of July in 1916 was especially festive; Cleveland's new City Hall had finally been completed and was dedicated on that day. Even though the site had been agreed upon in 1900, the land purchased during 1902/03, and Dyer's plans approved in 1906, actual construction did not begin until 1910.

The architecture — particularly the facade — is very similar to that of the County Court House. As major buildings flanking an esplanade at the south end of the Mall, they balance one another in both size and classical Beaux-Arts style. Sculptured figures were planned for the north and south cornices of City Hall (to correspond to those of the Court House). In fact, plaster models were prepared over a three-year period, from 1917 to 1920, by Herman Matzen and Walter Sinz, instructors at the Cleveland School of Art. Although these models were designed to represent the various departments of the city (health, recreation, safety, finance, law, utilities, and service) as well as industries (steel, textiles, shipbuilding, chemistry, electricity, and fisheries), the statues in granite were never completed.

The building's handsome interior contains marble floors, fluted columns, and vaulted spaces. The main entrance opens through a vestibule into a two-story great hall with a coffered ceiling that is lighted from above.

Archibald Willard's famous painting *The Spirit of '76*, done in 1912 specifically for display in City Hall, rests on a tripod/

stand on the main floor. (It has only just been removed for restoration, but will be on view again by October 1986.) A more recent painting entitled *The New Spirit of '76*, commissioned for America's Bicentennial in 1976, was painted by New York artist Carol Wald; the work is displayed adjacent to the first painting. Mural panels depicting scenes of Cleveland decorate the City Council chambers; the most famous of these, *Where Men and Minerals Meet*, was painted by Ivor Johns.

Figure 65. The mayor's private office as photographed in 1981. [43a]

Figure 66. The great hall, Cleveland City Hall. Flanking the two pillars at ground level in the center are the paintings *The Spirit of '76* (right, nearly obscured) and *The New Spirit of '76* (left). [39]

*Public Auditorium and Music Hall
(1922/1928)*
1220 East 6th Street
(Lakeside Avenue at East 6th)
J. Harold MacDowell, city architect
(Public Auditorium);
Herman Kregelius, city architect
(Music Hall);
Frank R. Walker, consulting architect

The fourth building in the Group Plan, Cleveland's Public Auditorium was the largest and finest convention hall in the United States at the time of its opening on April 15, 1922. So appealing was it, that the Republican party chose to hold their National Convention there in the summer of 1924. Over 300 feet long, 215 feet wide, and 80 feet high, the Auditorium could accommodate up to 13,000 people; because no columns were used, the view from each seat is unobstructed. The curtain for the stage was the largest ever made, weighing over forty tons with its counterweights.

Mounted on an elevator was a massive pipe organ, said to be the finest in the world, that could be raised or lowered in front of the stage.

The exhibition hall in the basement contained open space for large exhibits as well as forty columns to support the main floor of the Auditorium.

Interest in a large, public auditorium originated in the last quarter of the nineteenth century and was revived in 1909, when Cleveland held its great Industrial Exposition. A temporary structure was built on what is now the site of City Hall; but when it was torn down following the Exposition, civic-minded citizens agitated for a permanent building. They formed the Committee of One Hundred Organizations (116 groups, over 200,000 members) that was responsible for the passage in 1916 of a sizable bond issue to underwrite the project, which was to cost nearly $11 million by the time of its

completion. Because of World War I,
however, construction was delayed until
1920.

Artist David Lithgow of Albany, New
York, painted two large murals in the
auditorium area and three smaller over-
door paintings in the lounge area.

By 1927 an even larger facility was
needed, and the architects extended
their design to include north and south
additions that carry out the Italian
Renaissance style of the original building.
The north wing contained a new lobby,
executive offices, three small halls, and
a ballroom. The south wing, designated
the Music Hall, housed a 3,000-seat
theater whose walls contained niches and
other embellishments reminiscent of
Moorish architecture.

The Music Hall opened in 1928.

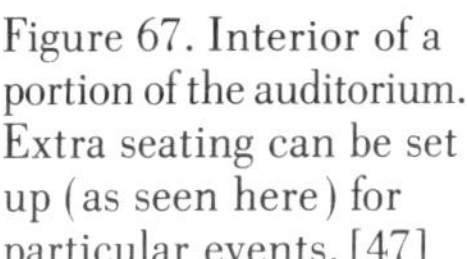

Figure 67. Interior of a portion of the auditorium. Extra seating can be set up (as seen here) for particular events. [47]

Federal Reserve Bank of Cleveland (1923)
Superior Avenue at East 6th Street
Walker & Weeks, architects

The design of this twelve-story foursquare building was intended to parallel the great palazzi in Florence, which were built as fortress-residences for the elite. A magnificent Italian Renaissance-style interior that includes marble floors, Sienese marble-faced walls and pillars, vaulted ceilings ornamented with gold gilt, and detailed ironwork belies the sober formality of the building's exterior.

Two stone sculptures, representing *Security* and *Integrity,* flank the entrance on East 6th Street, while a colossal bronze figure representing *Energy* graces the Superior Avenue entrance. New York sculptor Henry Hering executed all three. Many of the ornately decorated ceilings were hand painted by Joseph Sturdy of Chicago; and in the lobby, a mural panel depicting steel-making in Cleveland mills

was painted by Cora Holden, artist and teacher of painting at the Cleveland School of Art. Portraits of Alexander Hamilton and Robert Morris, by Clevelander Alonzo Kimball, hang in the elegant reception room on the eighth floor.

It was a distinct honor in 1913, when the Federal Reserve System had been inaugurated, for Cleveland to have been chosen as headquarters for the Fourth District (of twelve Federal Reserve Districts in the United States). Obviously,

Figure 69. Main entrance on East 6th Street. The bases of the sculptures representing *Security* and *Integrity* at one time had been equipped with light cannons; these were removed, however, about 1941. [133a]

Figure 68. Superior Avenue entrance with seated sculpture of *Energy*, executed by Henry Hering ca. 1922-23. [129b]

Figure 70. Detail of main entrance. The emblem at the top is the seal of the Fourth Federal Reserve District. Replicas of classical coins in the metopes refer to the ancient origin of modern currency. [133d]

Cleveland's selection enhanced the importance of the city as a financial center, and the handsome building designed by Frank Walker and Harry Weeks reflects that development. Over $8 million was expended for construction and interior accoutrements during 1922/23, but the result was that the building harmonized well with those in the Group Plan.

The bank vault is the world's largest, with a steel door that is nearly five feet thick. It required a crew of twelve men two days and nights to unload the 300-ton door from the railroad car that brought it to Cleveland, and it took four days and nights to move it from the station to the bank — a distance of one mile!

A prevalent misconception is that the bank is a governmental institution, not open to the public. Such is not the case: the bank is privately owned (by the banks of the Fourth District), and even though the United States Government is the largest depositor, individuals may purchase savings bonds or Treasury bills during banking hours. Visitors are invited to tour this beautiful, remarkably well-preserved building Monday through Friday, by appointment.

Figure 71. Interior views of the Federal Reserve Bank showing a portion of the magnificent main banking room [134] and the large mural by Cora Holden that depicts steel production in Cleveland [137].

Union Trust Building (1924)
East 9th Street, bounded by Euclid and
Chester Avenues
Graham, Anderson, Probst & White,
architects

With its twenty stories, this was the
second largest office building in the world,
and its striking three-story banking hall
was without equal in the United States.
Elegant Corinthian columns of marble
brought from Italy mark the perimeter
of the 50-foot-wide lobby, and a barrel-
vaulted ceiling not only adds a graceful
cover but provides ample skylights as well.

Murals in the lunettes at the entrance-
ways of the building and in the rotunda
were painted by Jules Guerin of New
York, who had also done the murals for
New York's Pennsylvania Station.

An unusual event occurred in 1923,
when the building was under construction.
During July, 2,500 bankers were in town
for the American Institute of Banking

Figure 72. The Euclid Avenue entrance of the Union Trust Building, which later became Union Commerce Bank [138]. Below is the architects' presentation rendering for the building, ca. 1922 [139].

Convention, and the visitors drove 250 automobiles through the lobby on an inspection tour.

On May 19, 1924, the building, with more than thirty acres of floor space, opened for business. The Union Trust Company's banking facilities occupied five floors; various offices, the remainder. In 1930 the Cleveland Stock Exchange established its headquarters in the building.

A reorganization of the bank in 1938 resulted in a name change to the Union Bank of Commerce; in succeeding years, however, the name became simply Union Commerce Bank. In 1983 the bank merged with Huntington National Bank and became Huntington Bank of Northeast Ohio. The most recent name adopted (October 1984) is Huntington National Bank.

Figure 73. Details of the splendid banking hall, in 1924 the largest in the United States. Above: Jules Guerin's mural entitled *Architecture and Engineering* [140f]. Top right: The main floor, looking toward grand staircase and Guerin murals [140c]. Lower right: View from mezzanine of the coffered ceiling and capitals [140b].

Cleveland Public Library (1925)
325 Superior Avenue
Walker & Weeks, architects

As early as 1853, a small library was set up at Central High School. Fourteen years later, an Ohio law authorized a tax (for cities over 20,000) to provide for the establishment of public libraries. The ensuing years saw many transient sites for the growing library that had begun at the high school. In 1912 the citizens of Cleveland voted for a $2 million bond issue to provide a new library, which would be an integral part of the Group Plan.

A competition for the design of the building was held in 1916. Of eight architectural firms that were asked to submit plans, only three were from Cleveland: Walker & Weeks (who were selected), Hubbell and Benes (who had designed The Cleveland Museum of Art), and Abram Garfield.

Construction began in 1922, after the citizens voted an additional $2 million bond issue to meet increased costs, and the name changed from the Public Library of the School District of the City of Cleveland to Cleveland Public Library. Forty-seven miles of shelving made it the third largest library in the country.

The architects were successful in designing a five-story marble building both to serve the purposes of a library and to harmonize with other buildings in the Group Plan — particularly the Federal Building. The furniture throughout was also designed by the architects to blend with the architecture. Because of the need for a maximum amount of daylight, the window area they designed is about forty percent greater than that of the Federal Building.

Pink marble floors and Italian marble walls, staircases, and balustrades, as well as the vaulted lobby, reflect the classical Beaux-Arts style also adhered to in the

Court House and City Hall. An inner light court at the third- and fourth-floor levels is enhanced by surrounding brickwork in the style of early Florentine architecture.

Edwin H. Blashfield, who had also painted a mural in the County Court House, made the studies for mural paintings representing the subjects of Music, Art, Literature, Poetry, Drama, and Architecture.

In an advertisement they had placed in the *Cleveland Plain Dealer* of May 10, 1925 (marking the opening of the new building), the painting contractors said: *As Athens prided itself on its Acropolis, as Rome boasted its Coliseum, so does Cleveland look upon its new Public Library. It is truly a beautiful building, a fitting shrine for its treasures, and will serve as the community's center of information and source of knowledge for many years to come. In realizing this dream, the people of Cleveland have built wisely and well.*

Figure 74. The west staircase in the Library's main hall. [61f]

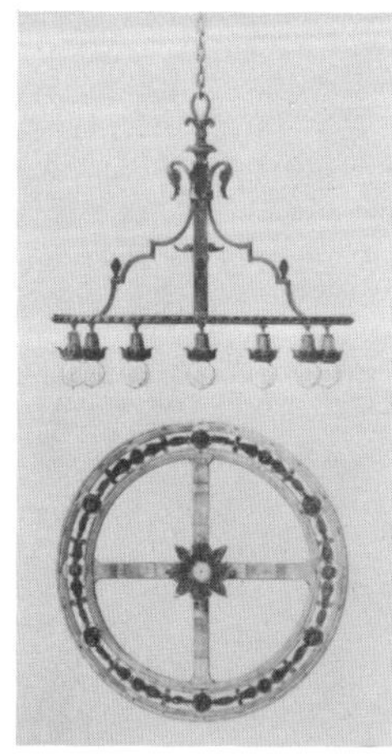

Figure 75. Sketches for Library light fixtures designed by Sterling Bronze Company, New York. 1924. [61g, a, b, i]

*Board of Education Headquarters Building
(1931)*
1385 East 3rd Street
Walker & Weeks, architects

Completing the east side of the Mall in the Group Plan, this six-story sandstone building faced the Mall, but its "back" door became the main entrance, on East 6th Street. The site, the building, and the landscaping cost $2,645,000 in 1929/30 when construction took place. On November 13, 1931, the move from the Standard Trust Bank Building to the new building was completed; in ten days of moving, 175 truckloads of material had been transferred.

A two-story lobby with marble floor and bluish-green Italian marble pillars was decorated with two 12-by-16-foot mural panels painted by Cleveland artist Cora Holden (who had earlier painted a mural in the Federal Reserve Bank Building). The subjects are: *Progress of Education* and *Branches of Education.* The auditorium stage is flanked by decorative panels by another Cleveland artist, Rolf Stoll.

An unusual feature of the third-floor library is a fireplace made from bricks of the old Rockwell School, the Board's Headquarters for twenty-two years.

Early in 1932 a statue of Abraham Lincoln, executed by Cleveland sculptor Max Kalish, was dedicated and placed near the entranceway facing the Mall. Inscribed on its base is the Gettysburg Address. A gift of Cleveland's school children, the statue had been financed by the children's pennies.

As one of the last buildings in the Group Plan to be erected over a period of two decades, the Board of Education Headquarters attests to the spirit engendered by the architects of the Plan. They, along with civic leaders in Cleveland, believed that the city's public buildings need not be merely utilitarian quarters but also places of beauty that embody much of our cultural heritage.

Figure 76. The west facade of the Board of Education Building facing the Mall [64a]. The sculpture near the entrance depicts Abraham Lincoln delivering the Gettysburg Address (detail, left).

J ust when Cleveland had sunk to the lowest point of its existence, two major events occurred, at the end of 1980, that augured well for the city's future. Those who followed the intricacies of city planning with an insider's perception recognized that suddenly there was new energy. During the following five years, various other events proved that the public and private energies of the city were joining forces in response to the city's problems, and doing so in a manner that readily called to mind the earlier commitment at the turn of the century.

In December of 1980, having made the major decision to build new corporate headquarters in downtown Cleveland, The Standard Oil Company (Sohio), and specifically its chairman, Alton W. Whitehouse, Jr., asked the firm of van Dijk, Johnson & Partners as well as the city's Planning Commission to study the pros and cons of three possible sites on Public Square. Two were easily eliminated: one facing the northwest quadrant of the Square seemed uninteresting; the other, on the northeast quadrant, supported two major buildings — the Engineers Building (which in 1910 was the first union-funded building to be built in America) and the Society National Bank Building (one of America's first steel-frame buildings, and a pivotal work by the architect John Wellborn Root that was important in the evolution of his partnership with Burnham, the mastermind behind the city's earlier Group Plan). While the trapezoidal shape of the third, and finally chosen, site presented a considerable challenge, the resulting Sohio Building responds admirably to the demands of its setting.

The angled, eight-story facade ingeniously veils the fact that Euclid and Superior Avenues are at two quite different levels, yet its height harmonizes happily with the scale of the buildings surrounding the square. And by placing the north-side facade of the tower portion of the building virtually in the center of the space between the Old Federal Building (now the Federal Court House) and Cleveland Public Library, Sohio finally created that long-desired focal point at the southern end of the Mall that had so plagued the planners seventy years earlier. But most important, the unusual shape of the building is an asset, since ingeniously it becomes the linch-pin linking the great Beaux-Arts space of the Mall with Public Square and the Terminal Tower. Thus, the two grand, and at times conflicting, ideas of an earlier day finally become interrelated because of a planning effort by a great private corporation working closely with the city's officials. And this close interaction between the private-public sectors of Cleveland would seem to be emerging as the significant hope for Cleveland's future.

Simultaneously, it was finally accepted that even though the winds blowing in from Lake Erie make the winter months nearly intolerable (in Chicago the winds come instead from the land — an essential factor in explaining that city's effective shore planning), the lakefront was, nonetheless, an ideal area to respond to the needs of the people. The immense success of the Great Lakes Exposition of 1936-37 had made that point so well that even though many self-serving proposals were made in the intervening years, the saving of that land for the people had become increasingly a leitmotif of the city's planning. Thus in 1985 — and could there be a more appropriate celebration of the 150th anniversary of the City's incorporation? — significant funds were allocated for the first phase of an impressive new plan that is projected to include a marina, an aquarium, a maritime museum, and shops, all appropriate for a waterfront area. Clearly, there is hope for the future. That scheme, it should be noted, was carefully designed to become an extension of the earlier Plan; simultaneously, it would be a gateway into the city from the lake, even as it would become, as had been the case with the 1936-37 Exposition, the northern terminus of the Beaux-Arts space. And a long-standing problem would be solved: the railroad tracks would be spanned.

During these same few years since 1980, other major events have occurred, or are yet to happen, which can only have a tremendous impact upon the city's overall appearance: the redesigning of the buildings surrounding Terminal Tower, done with an energy and imagination quite as exciting as those of the earlier Van Sweringen brothers; the domed stadium, appropriately sited for practical reasons; the various projected developments along Euclid Avenue, from Playhouse Square to the area around the Cleveland Clinic to University Circle — all designed to revitalize a sad street that failed to make the transition from a grand residential progression to the neighborhood needs of the late twentieth century; and the much-needed examination of the city's transportation patterns.

Obviously, therefore, studying the experience of an earlier generation is hardly an academic exercise. As much can be learned from understanding how a big idea was envisioned as from recognizing how varied can be the forces for accomplishment and for obstruction — because, understandably, planning for a city can be just as complicated as the many constituent elements of its citizenry. Ultimately, the people are the life of the city, and it is they who provide both the incentive and the resources for achievement in planning responsibly for the city's future.

E.H.T.

1. *World's Columbian Exposition, Chicago, Illinois*
Building supervisor: Daniel H. Burnham, Chicago.
1a. Court of Honor, 1893.
1b. The Farmer's Bridge Leading to the Agricultural
Hall on the South Side of the Grand Basin, 1893.
(After Ives 1893, pp. 139, 173)

2. *Cleveland Chamber of Commerce Building*
Completed 1898, now demolished. Architects: Peabody
& Stearns, Boston. The Newspaper Enterprise
Association.

3. *Location of Public Buildings and Improvement of the
Lakefront, Cleveland*
Lithographic copy of site plan, 25 x 28 inches, dated
January 2, 1900. Prepared by Cleveland Chamber of
Commerce, Committee on the Grouping Plan. Civil
engineer: C. W. Pratt. Western Reserve Historical
Society, Cleveland.

4. *The Group Plan of the Public Buildings of the City of
Cleveland (Scheme B)*
Photo-enlargement of site plan, 57-3/4 x 30 inches, 1903.
Prepared by Public Board of Supervision (Group Plan
Commission: Daniel H. Burnham, John M. Carrère, and
Arnold W. Brunner). Western Reserve Historical
Society, Cleveland.

5. *Report on the Group Plan of the Public Buildings of
the City of Cleveland Ohio*
Published report, 21-1/2 x 14-3/4 inches, 1903. Authors/
Architects: Group Plan Commission. Cleveland Public
Library.

6. *The Group Plan*
Presentation rendering of section through esplanade,
taken east and west, looking south towards Court House,
City Hall, the Mall, Federal Building, and Public Library.
Pen and ink wash on heavy paper, 13-1/4 x 98 inches,
1903. Prepared by Group Plan Commission. Western
Reserve Historical Society, Cleveland.

7. *Report on the Group Plan of the Public Buildings of
the City of Cleveland Ohio (2nd edition)*
Published report, 20 x 15 inches, 1907. Authors/
Architects: Group Plan Commission. Cleveland Public
Library.

8. *Proposed Union Station at North End of Mall*
Presentation rendering, pen and gouache on heavy
paper, 32-3/4 x 74-1/2 inches, ca. 1914. Signed: L.L.
C.B. Del[v?]; L.R. Graham, Burnham & Co. Arch'ts.
Prepared by Graham, Burnham & Co., Chicago. Western
Reserve Historical Society, Cleveland.

9. *The Group Plan*
Presentation rendering of detail elevation of fountain at
south end of Mall, with treatment of gardens, terraces,
formal trees, and reflecting pool of water. Pen and ink
wash on heavy paper, 31 x 52-1/2 inches, 1903. Prepared
by Group Plan Commission. Western Reserve Historical
Society, Cleveland.

10. *The Group Plan*
Page from *Report on the Group Plan...*, 22-3/4 x 16
inches, 1903. Detail elevation and detail plan for fountain at south end of Mall. Western Reserve Historical
Society, Cleveland.

11. *The Group Plan (Scheme B)*
Presentation rendering of detail plan for fountain at
north end of Mall, between Court House and City Hall.
Pen and ink wash on heavy paper, 24-1/4 x 31-7/8
inches, 1903. Prepared by Group Plan Commission.
Western Reserve Historical Society, Cleveland.

12. *The Group Plan*
Page from *Report on the Group Plan...*, 22-3/4 x 16
inches, 1903. Detail elevation and detail plan for fountain at north end of Mall, between Court House and
City Hall. Western Reserve Historical Society, Cleveland.

13. *The Group Plan*
Pages from *Report on the Group Plan...*, each 22-3/4
x 16 inches, 1903.
13a. Illustrations of executed work, showing various
features suggested in proposed treatment of landscaping and in architecture of the Group Plan.
13b. Additional illustrations of executed work.

14. *The Group Plan*
Photocopy mounted on cardboard: map of business
section of Cleveland, indicating territory to be included
in the Group Plan scheme and land to be acquired,
60-1/2 x 33-3/8 inches, 1903. Prepared by Group Plan
Commission. Western Reserve Historical Society,
Cleveland.

15. *Public Square, Cleveland*
Photograph: view from west side of Square looking east
towards U.S. Post Office foundations and Mall site, ca.
1905. (After *Glimpses of Greater Cleveland*, 1905)

16. *U.S. Post Office, Custom House, and Court House
(Federal Building)*
Building completed 1910. Architect: Arnold W. Brunner.
16a. Photograph of south entrance on Superior Avenue,
1986.
16b. Photograph: view from Public Square looking
northeast, ca. 1910. Cleveland Public Library.

17. *Federal Building*
Drawing of west elevation (Public Square elevation),
pencil on paper, 23-1/2 x 35-5/8 inches, ca. 1905.
Western Reserve Historical Society, Cleveland.

18. *Place de la Concorde, Paris*
Photograph from *Report on the Group Plan...*, 1903.

19. *The Group Plan*
Photograph of section through the Mall, taken east and
west, looking south and showing Federal Building and
Public Library. Prepared by Group Plan Commission.
(After *Report on the Group Plan...*, 1903)

20. *Federal Building*
20a. Photograph (1984) of free-standing sculptural
figure, *Jurisprudence*, at west end of south facade;
executed by Daniel Chester French, 1912.
20b. Photograph (1984) of free-standing sculptural
figure, *Commerce*, at east end of south facade; executed
by Daniel Chester French, 1912.

21. *The City of Cleveland, Supported by Federal Power,
Welcomes the Arts Bearing the Plan for the New Civic
Center*
Color photograph (1986) of oil painting in the Federal
Building, 7-1/2 x 5 feet. Painted by William H. Low,
ca. 1910.

22. *Cuyahoga County Court House*
Building completed 1912. Architects: Lehman & Schmitt,
Cleveland. Photograph of main entrance on Lakeside
Avenue, 1986. Western Reserve Historical Society,
Cleveland.

23. *Hôtel de Cité, Nancy, France*
Photograph of main facade. (After André Hallays, *Nancy*
[Paris: Librarie Renouard, 1906], p. 90)

24. *Cuyahoga County Court House*
South elevation, drawing no. 11, ink on linen, 25 x 59-3/4
inches, dated September 27, 1905. Cuyahoga County
Archives, Cleveland.

25. *Cuyahoga County Court House*
Longitudinal section, drawing no. 15, ink on linen,
26-1/2 x 59-3/4 inches, dated September 27, 1905, and
revised May 9, 1906. Cuyahoga County Archives,
Cleveland.

26. *Cuyahoga County Court House*
West elevation, drawing no. 14, ink on linen, 25 x 40-3/8
inches, dated September 27, 1905, revised May 9, 1906.
Cuyahoga County Archives, Cleveland.

27. *Cuyahoga County Court House*
Scale detail of southwest corner, drawing no. 58, ink on
linen, 93 x 47-7/8 inches, dated September 27, 1905.
Cuyahoga County Archives, Cleveland.

28. *Cuyahoga County Court House*
28a. Central motive of south front, drawing no. 56, ink
on linen, 93 x 47-7/8 inches, dated September 27, 1905.
Cuyahoga County Archives, Cleveland.
28b. Photograph (sideview, 1986) of central motive.
Western Reserve Historical Society, Cleveland.

29. *Cuyahoga County Court House*
29a. Photograph of south entrance with sculptural
figures. Left to right: Archbishop of Canterbury Stephen
Langton, Simon de Montfort, Edward I, John Hampden,
John Somers, and William Murray. Sculptures flanking
entrance: Thomas Jefferson and Alexander Hamilton.
Sculptors: Herbert Adams (Langton and de Montfort),
Daniel Chester French (Edward I and Hampden), and
Karl Bitter (Somers, Murray, Jefferson, and Hamilton).
Western Reserve Historical Society, Cleveland.
29b. Photograph (1980) of seated sculptural figure,
Thomas Jefferson, executed by Karl Bitter, 1909-11.
29c. Photograph of seated sculptural figure, *Alexander
Hamilton,* at south entrance; executed by Karl Bitter,
1909-11.

30. *Cuyahoga County Court House*
Photograph of interior, 1986. Designer: Charles
Schweinfurth, Cleveland, 1912. Western Reserve
Historical Society, Cleveland.

31. *Cuyahoga County Court House*
Photograph of ornamental bronze gate, 1986. Western
Reserve Historical Society, Cleveland.

32. *Cleveland City Hall*
Completed 1916. Architect: J. Milton Dyer, Cleveland.
Photograph: view from the southwest on Lakeside
Avenue. Western Reserve Historical Society, Cleveland.

33. *Cleveland City Hall*
33a. Preliminary sketch for south facade, pencil on
paper, 16-1/2 x 28 inches, ca. 1905.
33b. Preliminary sketch for south facade, pencil on
paper, 14-3/4 x 28-1/2 inches, ca. 1905.
33c. Preliminary sketch for south facade, pencil on
paper, 17 x 28-1/2 inches, ca. 1905.
The City of Cleveland.

34. *Cleveland City Hall*
Longitudinal section, ink and wash on heavy paper,
23 x 63-3/4 inches, ca. 1905. Western Reserve Historical
Society, Cleveland.

35. *Cleveland City Hall*
Preliminary sketch for side elevation, pencil on paper,
14-1/4 x 29 inches. The City of Cleveland.

36. *Cleveland City Hall*
Side elevation, ink and wash on paper, 22-1/2 x 45-3/4
inches, dated May 19, 1906. Signed: J. Milton Dyer;
S. G. Gladwin, V.P.; Edward A. Robert, CLK. Western
Reserve Historical Society, Cleveland.

37. *Cleveland City Hall*
Southwest corner of south elevation, drawing no. 107,
ink on linen, 85-1/2 x 46-1/2 inches, dated October 21,
1911. The City of Cleveland.

38. *Cleveland City Hall*
38a. Longitudinal section through vestibule looking
north, pencil on paper, 21-1/4 x 32-1/2 inches, ca. 1911.
38b. Section through vestibule looking north, pencil
on paper, 14-5/8 x 27-1/2 inches, ca. 1911.
The City of Cleveland.

39. *Cleveland City Hall*
Photograph of grand hall, 1980.

40. *Cleveland City Hall*
Detail of grand hall, drawing no. 111, ink on linen,
36-3/8 x 50-1/2 inches, dated July 22, 1912. The City
of Cleveland.

41. *Cleveland City Hall*
One and one-half inch scale drawing of Central [Grand]
Hall, showing marble work; ink on linen, 57-3/8 x 40-1/2
inches, dated July 22, 1912. The City of Cleveland.

42. *Cleveland City Hall*
Details of bronze clock in public
lobbies of waterworks and auditors departments, ink
on linen, 36 x 51-1/2 inches, dated March 16, 1914.
The City of Cleveland.

43. *Cleveland City Hall*
43a. Photograph of mayor's private office, 1981.
43b. Preliminary sketch for mayor's private office, east
elevation, pencil on paper, 21-1/4 x 27-3/4 inches,
ca. 1911.
43c. Preliminary sketch for mayor's private office, east
elevation, pencil on paper, 13-5/8 x 24-3/4 inches,
ca. 1911.
43d. Preliminary sketch for mayor's private office, east
elevation, pencil on paper, 13-5/8 x 20-1/2 inches,
ca. 1911.
43e. Detail drawing of ceiling of mayor's private office,
pencil on paper, 21 x 25-1/2 inches, ca. 1911.
The City of Cleveland.

44. *Public Auditorium*
Completed 1922. Architects: J. Harold MacDowell, city
architect, and Frank R. Walker, consultant. Photograph
of east facade, 1986.

45. *Chamber of Commerce Building with "Vote for Public
Hall Banner,"* ca. 1916. The Newspaper Enterprise
Association.

46. *Public Auditorium*
46a. East elevation, pencil and ink on linen, 37-1/4 x
83-3/4 inches, ca. 1917.
46b. North and south elevations, pencil and ink on
linen, 37-1/2 x 84 inches, ca. 1917.
The City of Cleveland.

47. *Public Auditorium*
Photograph of interior, 1986. Western Reserve Historical
Society, Cleveland.

48. *Public Auditorium*
Second-floor plan, pencil and ink on linen, 37-3/4 x
81-3/4 inches, dated March 7, 1917. The City of Cleveland.

49. *North Wing Addition for Public Auditorium*
Completed 1928. Architects: Herman Kregelius, city
architect, and Frank R. Walker, consultant.
49a. Blueprint for north elevation, no. 2612, 26 x 42
inches, dated March 9, 1927.
49b. Blueprint for east and west elevations, no. 2613,
26 x 42 inches, dated March 9, 1927.
The City of Cleveland.

50. *South Wing Addition for Public Hall (Music Hall)*
Completed 1928. Architects: Herman Kregelius, city
architect, and Frank R. Walker, consultant. Blueprint
for south elevation, 26 x 42 inches, dated March 9,
1927. The City of Cleveland.

51. *Site Plan of Proposed Veteran's Building at North End
of Mall*
Hand-colored photocopy of line drawing, 15-3/8 x 10-1/4
inches, ca. 1922. Architects: Hubbell and Benes,
Cleveland. Cleveland Public Library.

52. *Cleveland Public Library*
Completed 1925. Architects: Walker and Weeks,
Cleveland. Photograph of south facade, 1986.

53. *Old City Hall*
Photograph of site chosen for future Cleveland Public
Library, ca. 1912. Cleveland Public Library.

54. *Cleveland Public Library*
Pencil rendering, 15-1/2 x 21-1/4 inches, ca. 1917.
Western Reserve Historical Society, Cleveland.

55. *Cleveland Public Library*
55a. Booklet: "Program of Competition for Proposed
Main Library Building in the City of Cleveland," 10-5/8
x 7-3/4 inches, dated 1916.
55b. Competition design. Architects: Holabird and
Roche, Chicago. Photograph of elevation to Superior
Street, dated 1917.
55c. Competition design. Architects: Holabird and
Roche, Chicago. Photograph of transverse section
looking north, dated 1917.
55d. Competition design. Architects: Allen and Collens,
Boston. Photograph of Superior Avenue elevation, 1917.
55e. Competition design. Architects: Allen and Collens,
Boston. Photograph of transverse section, 1917.
55f. Competition design. Architect: Abram Garfield,
Cleveland. Photograph of elevation to Superior Street,
1917.
55g. Competition design. Architect: Abram Garfield,
Cleveland. Photograph of section through north-south
axis, 1917.
55h. Competition design. Architect: Robert D. Kohn,
New York. Photograph of elevation to Superior Street,
1917.
55i. Competition design. Architect: Robert D. Kohn,
New York. Photograph of section through north-south
axis, 1917.
55j. Competition design. Architect: J. R. Pope, New
York. Photograph of elevation to Superior Street, 1917.
55k. Competition design. Architect: J. R. Pope, New
York. Photograph of section through east-west axis,
1917.
55l. Competition design. Architects: Walker and Weeks,
Cleveland. Photograph of Superior Avenue elevation,
1917.
55m. Competition design. Architects: Walker and Weeks,
Cleveland. Photograph of section, 1917.
55n. Competition design. Architect: Edward L. Tilton,
New York. Photograph of elevation to Superior Street,
1917.
55o. Competition design. Architect: Edward L. Tilton,
New York. Photograph of section through east-west
axis, 8 x 10 inches, 1917.
55p. Competition design. Architects: Hubbell and Benes,
Cleveland. Photograph of Superior Avenue elevation,
1917.
55q. Competition design. Architects: Hubbell and Benes,
Cleveland. Photograph of section through north-south
axis, 1917.
Cleveland Public Library.

56. *Cleveland Public Library*
56a. Competition design. Architects: Hubbell and Benes,
Cleveland. Photo-enlargement of Superior Avenue
elevation, 18 x 23-3/4 inches, 1917. Cleveland Public
Library.
56b. Competition design. Architects: Hubbell and Benes,
Cleveland. Photo-enlargement of section through
north-south axis, 18 x 23-3/4 inches, 1917. Cleveland
Public Library.
56c. Competition design. Architects: Hubbell and Benes,
Cleveland. Photo-enlargement of plan for first story,
18 x 23-3/4 inches, 1917. Cleveland Public Library.

57. *Cleveland Public Library*
57a. Blueprint for south elevation, sheet no. 11, 27-5/8
x 40 inches, dated August 16, 1919. Prepared by Walker
and Weeks, Cleveland. Cleveland Public Library.
57b. Photocopy of south elevation, sheet no. 11, 13-1/2
x 19-3/8 inches, dated April 21, 1923. Western Reserve
Historical Society, Cleveland.
57c. Photocopy of north elevation, sheet no. 13, 13-3/4
x 19-1/2 inches, dated April 21, 1923. Western Reserve
Historical Society, Cleveland.

58. *Cleveland Public Library*
Aerial photograph looking south from Mall towards
Cleveland Public Library and the Federal Building, 1986.

59. *Place de Louis XV (now Place de la Concorde), Paris*
Bookplate II from Comte de Fels, *Ange-Jacques Gabriel
1698-1782*, (Paris: Emile-Paul, 1912): engraving of view
looking towards Rue Royale, 14-1/2 x 23 inches.
Architect: Ange-Jacques Gabriel, French (1698-1782).
The Cleveland Museum of Art Library.

60. *Cleveland Public Library*
60a. Photocopy of floor plans for 1st through 3rd floors,
32 x 10-1/2 inches, ca. 1925. Cleveland Public Library.
60b. Photocopy of section B.B., sheet no. 16, 13-1/2 x
19-1/4, dated April 21, 1923. Western Reserve Historical
Society, Cleveland.
60c. Photocopy of sections E.E. — L.L., sheet no. 19,
13-5/8 x 19-3/8 inches, dated April 21, 1923. Western
Reserve Historical Society, Cleveland.

61. *Cleveland Public Library*
Photographs of sketches for lights and light fixtures
designed by Sterling Bronze Company, New York.
61a. Reading room light fixtures, 1924.
61b. Light fixture at main entrance, 1924.
61c. Zodiac globe in entrance hall, 1924.
61d. Zodiac globe in entrance hall, ca. 1930.
61e. Lanterns for entrance hall at stairs, 1924.
61f. Fixture at bottom of west staircase.
61g. Chandelier for Brett Hall, 1924.
61h. Light fixture in Treasure Room, 1924.
61i. Light fixture for John G. White [Collection] Room,
1924.
Cleveland Public Library.

62. *Cleveland Public Library*
Pages advertising the Library's use of Georgia marble,
11-3/8 x 8-5/8 inches. Cleveland Public Library.

63. *Cleveland Public Library*
Photograph of arched window in Brett Hall, main floor.
Cleveland Public Library.

64. *Board of Education Headquarters Building*
Completed 1931. Architects: Walker and Weeks,
Cleveland.
64a. Photograph of west facade, view from Mall, 1986.
64b. Photograph of east facade, view from East 6th
Street, 1986.

65. *Board of Education Building*
65a. Elevation from the Mall, sheet no. 10, 26-3/4 x
46-1/2 inches, dated May 19, 1930.
65b. East elevation, sheet no. 12, 26-3/4 x 46-1/2 inches,
dated May 19, 1930.
65c. North and south elevations, sheet no. 11, 26-3/4
x 46-1/2 inches, dated May 19, 1930.
Cleveland City School District.

66. *Board of Education Building*
Drawing of vent grille over door no. 313 (Room 311),
pencil on paper, 42 x 51 inches, dated April 25, 1931.
Western Reserve Historical Society, Cleveland.

67. *Board of Education Building*
Drawing of plaster details in board room, sheet no. 239,
pencil on paper, 75-1/2 x 42 inches, dated February 25,
1931. Western Reserve Historical Society, Cleveland.

68. *Board of Education Building*
68a. Photograph: view looking towards the Mall from
building foundation, ca. 1930.
68b. Photograph: view looking towards newly completed
Board of Education Building from recently cleared Mall,
ca. 1931.
The Newspaper Enterprise Association.

69. *Board of Education Building*
Photograph of statue of Abraham Lincoln on Mall, west
of building. Executed by Max Kalish, ca. 1931.

70. *Cleveland Industrial Exposition*
Held 1927 on the Mall.
Photograph of decorative steel-framed "Tower of Jewels,"
1927. Contracted by Cleveland Electric Illuminating
Company. The Newspaper Enterprise Association.

71. *Site Plan of Group Plan Buildings Surrounding Mall*
Photocopy showing area originally proposed for Union
Station and for other possible uses to be determined
by future study, 16-1/2 x 11-1/16 inches, 1927. Prepared
by City of Cleveland. Cleveland Public Library.

72. *The Group Plan (1929)*
72a. Photograph of line drawing showing Mall and proposed lakefront public buildings, 1929. Prepared by
1929 Group Plan Commission. (After *The Clevelander* 4,
no. 4 [August 1929], p. 8)
72b. Photograph of plaster model for 1929 Plan in situ
in Fillous & Rupple Company, Cleveland, ca. 1929.
The Newspaper Enterprise Association.

73. *Proposed Building at South End of 1903 Group Plan*
Photograph of rendering, ca. 1913. Architects: Walker
and Weeks, Cleveland. Western Reserve Historical
Society, Cleveland.

74. *Proposed Bank Building at South End of 1903 Group
Plan*
Photograph of rendering, ca. 1921. Architects: Walker
and Weeks, Cleveland. Western Reserve Historical
Society, Cleveland.

75. *Proposed Building at South End of 1929 Group Plan*
Photograph of rendering, ca. 1930. Architects: Walker
and Weeks, Cleveland. Western Reserve Historical
Society, Cleveland.

76. *The Mall, with Sohio Building at South Terminus*
Aerial photograph, 1986. Air services provided by
John Zapone.

77. *Great Lakes Exposition*
Held 1936-37 along lakefront. Photographs, 1936.
77a. Aerial view looking south.
77b. Court of Presidents.
77c. The Mall.
The Newspaper Enterprise Association.

78. *The Group Plan (1903)*
Photograph of rendering of aerial view looking north
towards Lake Erie, 1903. (After *Report on the Group
Plan...*, 1903) Prepared by Group Plan Commission.
Cleveland Public Library.

79. *Proposed Union Station at North End of Mall*
Preliminary sketch, pencil on tissue paper, 15-1/2 x
25-7/8 inches, ca. 1914. Architects: Graham, Burnham
& Co., Chicago. Western Reserve Historical Society,
Cleveland.

80. *Proposed Union Station*
Preliminary sketch of site plan for landscaping in front
of station, pencil on tissue paper, 22-1/4 x 28 inches,
ca. 1914. Architects: Graham, Burnham & Co., Chicago.
Western Reserve Historical Society, Cleveland.

81. *Proposed Union Station*
Photo-enlarged rendering, hand-colored with ink wash
and chalk, 34-1/4 x 75-3/4 inches, ca. 1914-15.
Architects: Graham, Burnham & Co., Chicago. Western
Reserve Historical Society, Cleveland.

82. *Proposed Union Station (Scheme C1)*
Presentation drawing of buildings at north end of Mall,
pencil on paper, 16-3/4 x 33 inches, ca. 1915-16.
Architects: Graham, Burnham & Co., Chicago. Tower
City Archives, Forest City Enterprises, Cleveland.

83. *Proposed Union Station (Scheme C2)*
Presentation drawing of buildings at north end of Mall,
pencil on tissue paper, 16-7/8 x 32-3/4 inches, ca. 1915-16.
Architects: Graham, Burnham & Co., Chicago. Tower
City Archives, Forest City Enterprises, Cleveland.

84. *Proposed Union Station (Scheme C1)*
Site plan for north end of Mall including landscaping,
colored pencil on paper, 18 x 60-1/4 inches, ca. 1915-16.
Architects: Graham, Burnham & Co., Chicago. Tower
City Archives, Forest City Enterprises, Cleveland.

85. *Proposed Union Station (Scheme C2)*
Site plan for north end of Mall including landscaping,
colored pencil on paper, 19-3/4 x 64 inches, ca. 1915-16.
Architects: Graham, Burnham & Co., Chicago. Tower
City Archives, Forest City Enterprises, Cleveland.

86. *Proposed Union Station (Scheme C1)*
Front and side elevations and cross-section, pencil on
tissue paper, 26 x 40-1/2 inches, ca. 1915-16. Architects:
Graham, Burnham & Co., Chicago. Tower City Archives,
Forest City Enterprises, Cleveland.

87. *Proposed Union Station (Scheme C2)*
Side elevation and cross-section, pencil on tissue paper,
26 x 40-1/2 inches, ca. 1915-16. Architects: Graham,
Burnham & Co., Chicago. Tower City Archives, Forest
City Enterprises, Cleveland.

88. *Proposed Union Station (Scheme C1)*
Street-level plan, pencil on tissue paper, 26 x 40-1/2
inches, ca. 1915-16. Architects: Graham, Burnham & Co.,
Chicago. Tower City Archives, Forest City Enterprises,
Cleveland.

89. *Proposed Union Station (Scheme C2)*
Street-level plan, pencil on tissue paper, 26 x 40-1/2
inches, ca. 1915-16. Architects: Graham, Burnham & Co.,
Chicago. Tower City Archives, Forest City Enterprises,
Cleveland.

90. *Proposed Union Station (Scheme C2)*
Station-level plan, pencil on tissue paper, 26 x 40-1/2
inches, ca. 1915-16. Architects: Graham, Burnham & Co.,
Chicago. Tower City Archives, Forest City Enterprises,
Cleveland.

91. *The Van Sweringen Brothers*
Photographs, ca. 1929-30.
91a. Mantis J. Van Sweringen, 1881-1935.
91b. Oris P. Van Sweringen, 1879-1936.
The Newspaper Enterprise Association.

92. *Proposed Union Station, Public Square*
Photo-reproduction of rendering, 14-3/8 x 20-5/16, ca.
1918-19. Architects: Graham, Anderson, Probst & White,
Chicago. Tower City Archives, Forest City Enterprises,
Cleveland.

93. *Proposed Union Station, Public Square*
Presentation rendering showing round-about in place of
the square. Pencil and ink on paper, 23-1/2 x 26-11/16
inches, ca. 1920-23. Architects: Graham, Anderson,
Probst & White, Chicago. Tower City Archives, Forest
City Enterprises, Cleveland.

94. *Cleveland Union Terminals Company, Tower Building*
Completed 1929. Architects: Graham, Anderson, Probst
& White, Chicago. Photograph of plaster model, ca. 1923.

95. *Cleveland Union Terminals Company, Tower Building*
95a. Blueprint of Prospect Avenue elevation, sheet
no. 10, 70-14/16 x 42 inches, dated December 15, 1925.
95b. Blueprint of cross-section on axis looking west,
sheet no. 12, 70-12/16 x 42 inches, dated December 15,
1925.
95c. Blueprint for Public Square elevation, sheet no. 9,
71-1/16 x 41-7/8 inches, dated December 19, 1925.
Cleveland State University.

96. *Cleveland Union Terminals Development*
Photo-reproduction of plate from *Cleveland Union
Station: A Description of the New Passenger Facilities
and Surrounding Improvements*, 50th Anniversary
Facsimile Edition (Cleveland: Robert J. Liederbach
Publishing Co., 1979), pp. 16-17.

97. *Hotel Cleveland*
Completed 1918. Architects: George B. Post & Sons,
New York. Photograph: view from Superior Avenue
looking north, ca. 1918. The Newspaper Enterprise
Association.

98. *Hotel Cleveland and Southwest Corner of Public Square*
Aerial photograph, ca. 1918-19. Courtesy of Ress Realty
Co., Cleveland.

99. *Cleveland Union Terminal Site*
Aerial photograph, ca. 1923-24 (before construction).
Courtesy of Ress Realty Co., Cleveland.

100. *Cleveland Union Terminals Company*
Photograph of Tower Building under construction, ca.
1925-26. Architects: Graham, Anderson, Probst &
White, Chicago. The Newspaper Enterprise Association

101. *Cleveland Union Terminals Company*
Photograph of Tower Building with proposed office
tower complex drawn in, ca. 1928. Courtesy of Ress
Realty Co., Cleveland.

102. *Cleveland Union Terminals Company*
Photograph of concourse area under construction, ca.
1928. Courtesy of Ress Realty Co., Cleveland.

103. *Cleveland Union Terminals Company*
Photographs of Medical Arts and Builders Exchange
Buildings. Architects: Graham, Anderson, Probst &
White, Chicago.
103a. Under construction, ca. 1929-30.
103b. Construction completed on Medical Arts and
Builders Exchange Buildings and space cleared for
Midland Bank Building, ca. 1929-30.
Courtesy of Ress Realty Co., Cleveland.

104. *Cleveland Union Terminals Project*
Photograph of area in 1931. Courtesy of Ress Realty
Co., Cleveland.

105. *Terminal Tower*
Photographs of views towards Tower, dates uncertain.
105a. West from Euclid Avenue.
105b. Southwest from Superior Street.
105c. Southwest from northeast quadrant of Public
Square.
105d. South from Public Square.
105e. East from West 6th Street.
105f. From railroad tracks.
105g. From railroad tracks.
The Newspaper Enterprise Association.

106. *Terminal Tower, Cleveland*
Photograph, 13-7/16 x 10-1/4 inches, 1928, by Margaret
Bourke-White (1904-1971). The Cleveland Museum of
Art, Gift of Max and Betty Ratner, 85.76.

107. *Cleveland Union Terminal*
Color lithograph poster, "The New Union Terminal,
Cleveland New York Central Lines," 43-1/4 x 29-1/2
inches, ca. 1926. Artist: Leslie Ragan. Collection of A.G.
Edwards & Sons, Inc., St. Louis, Missouri.

108. *Cleveland Plain Dealer*
Special section on Union Terminal, dated June 29, 1930.
The Cleveland Museum of Art Library.

109. *Cleveland Union Terminal*
Photograph of main entrance, 1986.

110. *Cleveland Union Terminal*
110a. Lithograph of main entrance with doric columns,
18 x 23 inches, ca. 1923-24.
110b. Lithograph of main entrance with piers and ionic
capitals, 18 x 23 inches, ca. 1923-24.
110c. Lithograph of main entrance with piers and ionic
capitals, 18 x 23 inches, ca. 1923-24.
Tower City Archives, Forest City Enterprises, Cleveland.

111. *Cleveland Union Terminal*
Photograph of main entrance portico, 1986.

112. *Cleveland Union Terminal*
Light-fixture sketches. Designer: Sterling Bronze
Company, New York.
112a. Colored pencil on tissue: light fixtures at ends of
waiting rooms, 21 x 14 inches, ca. 1926-28.
112b. Colored pencil on tissue (in portfolio): light
fixture in main waiting room, 29-1/2 x 20-1/2 inches,
ca. 1926-28.
112c. Colored pencil on tissue: light fixture, 31-1/4 x
19 inches, ca. 1926-28.
Tower City Archives, Forest City Enterprises, Cleveland.

113. *Cleveland Union Terminal*
Light fixtures, ca. 1929. Designer: Sterling Bronze
Company, New York.
113a. Bronze and glass, diam. 36 inches.
113b. Bronze and glass, diam, 24 inches.
Tower City Archives, Forest City Enterprises, Cleveland.

114. *Cleveland Union Terminal*
114a. Arcade Directory, bronze, 85 x 31-1/4 inches.
114b. Railroad bench, wood, h. 42 inches, l. 30 feet.
114c. Two ticket windows, bronze, 38 x 22-1/2 inches.
114d. Railroad timetable, bronze, 68 x 56 inches.
114e. Ornamental grillwork for main concourse, bronze,
h. 42-3/4 inches, l. 19 feet.
114f. Ornamental grillwork for main concourse, bronze,
24-1/2 x 24-1/2 inches.
114g. Ornamental lintel for storefront in main concourse,
bronze, 6-1/2 x 94 inches.
114h. Ceiling grille with dragonfly motif for ticket lobby,
cast-iron, 52 x 21 inches.
Tower City Archives, Forest City Enterprises, Cleveland.

115. *Cleveland Union Terminal*
Coat rack, cast-iron top and bronze base, h. 73 inches.
Courtesy of Sand's Brass Door Restaurant & Lounge.

116. *Engineers Building*
Mailbox, bronze, 30 x 22-1/4 inches. Courtesy of Ress
Realty Co., Cleveland.

117. *Cleveland Union Terminal*
Photographs, 1986.
117a. Main concourse.
117b. Sand's Brass Door Restaurant & Lounge.
117c. Detail of grillwork in concourse area.

118. *New York Municipal Building, Manhattan*
Completed 1911-13. Architects: McKim, Mead & White.
Photograph, 1986.

119. *The Cleveland Trust Company*
Completed 1908. Architects: George B. Post & Sons,
New York. Photograph of exterior, 1986.

120. *The Cleveland Trust Company*
Plan for main facade in "Present and Current Work of
George B. Post & Sons," *The New York Architect* 3, no.
6 (June 1909). AmeriTrust Company, Cleveland.

121. *The Cleveland Trust Company*
Postcard, 5 x 7 inches, ca. 1908. AmeriTrust Company,
Cleveland.

122. *The Cleveland Trust Company*
Photograph of sculptural figures depicting "Allegori-
zation of the Main Springs of Wealth." Artist:
Karl Bitter.

123. *The Cleveland Trust Company*
123a. Photograph of Tiffany-style dome in banking hall,
1986.
123b. Photograph of dome and balcony with Francis
Millet's mural paintings, 1986.

124. *The Cleveland Trust Company*
Pamphlet: *The Development of Civilization in America:
Reproductions and Descriptions of a Series of Noteworthy
Paintings by Francis D. Millet in the Main Office of
The Cleveland Trust Company* (Text taken from an
article by Leila Mechlin in *World's Work*, December
1909). AmeriTrust Company, Cleveland.

125. *The Cleveland Trust Company*
Photograph of banking hall, 1986.

126. *The Cleveland Trust Company*
Photograph of banking hall, ca. 1908. (After *The New
York Architect* 3, no. 6 [June 1909])

127. *The Cleveland Trust Company*
Photographs, ca. 1910.

127a. President's office (now destroyed).
127b. Grotesque, *Miser Studying His Accounts*, in
president's office (now destroyed).
127c. Grotesque, *Miser Looking into His Money Box*, in
president's office (now destroyed).
127d. Grotesque, *Miser Figuring His Profits*, from
president's office (now destroyed).
AmeriTrust Company, Cleveland.

128. *Guardian Building (now National City Bank)*
Completed 1915-17. Architects: Walker and Weeks,
Cleveland. Photographs, 1986.
128a. Exterior elevation on Euclid Avenue.
128b. Interior banking hall looking north to grand
staircase.
128c. Marble staircase at north end of banking hall.
128d. Detail work and ceiling decoration in banking hall.

129. *Federal Reserve Bank of Cleveland*
Completed 1923. Architects: Walker and Weeks,
Cleveland.
129a. Photograph of exterior, 1985. Courtesy of van Dijk,
Johnson & Partners, architects, Cleveland.
129b. Photograph of Superior Avenue exterior, 1986.

130. *Federal Reserve Bank of Cleveland*
Rendering of proposed building; pencil, ink, and wash
on lithograph background on paper; 29-3/4 x 41-1/4
inches, ca. 1920. Western Reserve Historical Society,
Cleveland.

131. *Federal Reserve Bank of Cleveland*
131a. North (Rockwell Avenue) elevation, sheet no. 23,
ink on linen, 37-1/2 x 36-1/2 inches, dated 1921.
131b. West (East 6th Street) elevation, sheet no. 20,
ink on linen, 37-1/2 x 36-1/2 inches, dated 1921.
131c. South (Superior Avenue) elevation, sheet no. 21,
ink on linen, 37-1/2 x 36-1/4 inches, dated 1921.
Federal Reserve Bank of Cleveland.

132. *Federal Reserve Bank of Cleveland*
Presentation rendering of view of Superior Avenue
looking northeast towards bank. Pen, ink, and ink wash,
35 x 26 inches, dated 1921 (revised 1923). Federal
Reserve Bank of Cleveland.

133. *Federal Reserve Bank of Cleveland*
Photographs, 1980.
133a. Main entrance with sculptural figures, *Security*
and *Integrity;* executed by Henry Hering, 1922-23.
133b. *Security*
133c. *Integrity*
133d. Main entrance, detail work.

134. *Federal Reserve Bank of Cleveland*
Photograph of interior of main banking room, 1986.

135. *Federal Reserve Bank of Cleveland*
135a. Developed plan of dome, main banking room,
sheet no. 285, ink on linen, 36-1/4 x 3-1/4 inches.
135b. Elevation of end of main banking room, sheet
no. 284, ink on linen, 37 x 37-3/4 inches.
Federal Reserve Bank of Cleveland.

136. *Federal Reserve Bank of Cleveland*
Photograph of detail work in main banking room, 1986.
Ceiling painter: Joseph Sturdy, Chicago.

137. *Federal Reserve Bank of Cleveland*
Photograph of mural panel depicting steel-making in
Cleveland mills, painted ca. 1923. Artist: Cora Holden.

138. *Union Trust Building (now Huntington Bank)*
Completed 1924. Architects: Graham, Anderson, Probst
& White, Chicago. Photograph of exterior, 1985. Courtesy
of van Dijk, Johnson & Partners, architects, Cleveland.

139. *Union Trust Building*
Presentation rendering, hand-colored lithograph in
pencil, ink, and ink wash, 28-1/4 x 39-1/2 inches, ca.
1922. Huntington Bank, Cleveland.

140. *Union Trust Building*
Photographs, 1985.
140a. Main banking hall.
140b. Details of ceiling and capitals from mezzanine
level.
140c. Banking hall. Courtesy of van Dijk, Johnson &
Partners, architects, Cleveland.
140d. Skylight in rotunda. Courtesy of van Dijk,
Johnson & Partners, architects, Cleveland.
140e. Small mural by Jules Guerin, entitled *Industry
and Commerce.* Courtesy of van Dijk, Johnson & Partners,
architects, Cleveland.
140f. Large mural by Jules Guerin, entitled *Architecture
and Engineering.* Courtesy of van Dijk, Johnson &
Partners, architects, Cleveland.

Library of Congress Cataloging-in-Publication Data

Rarick, Holly M., 1961-
  Progressive vision.

  Catalogue of an exhibition organized by the museum.
  Bibliography: p.
  1. City planning — Ohio — Cleveland — Exhibitions.
2. Cleveland (Ohio) — Buildings, structures, etc. —
Exhibitions.   I. Cleveland Museum of Art.   II. Title.
NA9127.C6R37   1986   711'.4'0977132074017132
86-12950
ISBN 0-910386-86-2

Bibliography

Abercrombie, P. "Cleveland, A Civic Centre Project." *The Town Planning Review* 2 (April 1911): 131.

The Architecture of Cleveland: Twelve Buildings, 1836-1912. Selections from the Historic American Buildings Survey No. 12. Cleveland: Western Reserve Historical Society and Historic American Buildings Survey, 1973.

Bemis, Edward W. "Tom L. Johnson's Achievements as Mayor of Cleveland." *Review of Reviews* 43 (May 1911): 558-60.

Briggs, Herbert B. "Municipal Improvement, Cleveland." *The Inland Architect and News Record* 34 (August 1899): 4-5.

"Building of the Federal Reserve Bank of Cleveland." Cleveland: Federal Reserve Bank, 1937. Rev. 1938.

Burnham, Daniel H., Carrère, John M., and Brunner, Arnold W. *Report of the Group Plan of the Public Buildings of the City of Cleveland, Ohio.* Cleveland: Board of Supervision for Public Buildings and Ground, 1903. 2d ed. 1907.

Campen, Richard N. *Outdoor Sculpture in Ohio.* Chagrin Falls, Ohio: West Summit Press, 1980.

Cleveland. Board of Supervision for Public Buildings and Ground. *See* Burnham, Carrère, and Brunner 1903.

__________. Chamber of Commerce. Annuals for 1901, 1902, 1903, 1904.

__________. Chamber of Commerce. Committee on City Plan. "A City Plan for Greater Cleveland." 1923.

__________. Chamber of Commerce. Committee on City Plan. "Public Building Program for Cuyahoga County and the City of Cleveland." 1923.

__________. Chamber of Commerce. Committee on City Plan. "Vote 'Yes' on (1) the Mall Site, (2) the City-County Building." 1924.

__________. Chamber of Commerce. Grouping Plan Committee. "Progress of the Grouping Plan for Cleveland Public Buildings." 1904.

__________. City Plan Commission. "Cleveland Thorofare Plan." 1921.

__________. Division of Engineering and Construction. "Group Plan Data." 1931.

__________. Division of Information. "The Cleveland 'Mall' Plan." 1927.

"Cleveland as an Art Center." *Art and Archaeology* 16, nos. 4 & 5 (November 1923). Entire issue on Cleveland; many illustrations.

Cleveland Plain Dealer. August 16, 1902, p. 10. January 18, 1903, p. 4. February 5, 1903, p. 10. June 7, 1903, p. 9. "Union Terminal Section," June 29, 1930.

The Cleveland Trust Company: An Epitome of the Past, A Chronicle of the Present, A Promise of the Future. Cleveland, 1908.

Condon, George E. *Cleveland: The Best-Kept Secret.* Garden City, New York: Doubleday, 1967.

Court House: A Photographic Document [exhibition catalog]. Cleveland: Board of Cuyahoga County Commissioners, Cuyahoga County Archives, Criminal Justice Public Information Center, 1978.

C. R. "A New Civic Vision." *The Clevelander,* August 1929, 9, 31-32.

Croly, Herbert. "The United States Post Office, Custom House, and Court House, Cleveland, Ohio." *The Architectural Record* 29 (March 1911): 196.

Crowe, M. A. "The Heart of Cleveland; A Study in City Planning." *The Ohio Architect, Engineer, and Builder* 26 (November 1915): 9-17.

Cudell, F. E. "The Group Plan Question: A New Years' Study and a Warning." Cleveland: Public Administration Library, 1912.

Dennis, James M. *Karl Bitter: Architectural Sculptor, 1867-1915.* Madison, Milwaukee, and London: Univ. of Wisconsin Press, 1967.

Edwards, Frederick B. "The Grand Old Party's Convention Town." *The New York Tribune,* December 30, 1923, 5.

Glimpses of Greater Cleveland and Some Old-Time Views. Cleveland: Whitworth Brothers Company, 1905.

Haberman, Ian S. *The Van Sweringens of Cleveland.* Cleveland: Western Reserve Historical Society, 1979.

Hines, Thomas H. *Burnham of Chicago.* New York: Oxford University Press, 1974.

Hopkins (William R.) Papers, Ms. 3774, Western Reserve Historical Society, Cleveland.

Howe, Frederick C. "Cleveland, A City 'Finding Itself.'" *World's Work* 6 (October 1903): 3988-89.

__________. *The Confessions of a Reformer.* New York: C. Scribner's Sons, 1925.

Ives, Halsey, C. *The Dream City, A Portfolio of Photographic Views of the World's Columbian Exposition.* St. Louis: N. D. Thompson Publishing Co., 1893.

Johannesen, Eric. *Cleveland Architecture 1876-1976.* Cleveland: Western Reserve Historical Society, 1979.

__________. *From Town to Tower.* Cleveland: Western Reserve Historical Society, 1983.

Johnson, Tom L. *My Story.* New York: B. W. Huebsch, 1911.

Leedy, Walter C., Jr. "Cleveland's Terminal Tower — The Van Sweringens' Afterthought." Reprinted from *The Gamut* no. 8 (Winter 1983), published by Cleveland State University.

Make No Little Plans. Introduction and catalog by Michael G. Lawrence. Cleveland: Western Reserve Historical Society, 1980.

Mather, William G. "Dreams into Granite." *The Clevelander,* June 1926.

Rose, William Ganson. *Cleveland: The Making of a City.* Cleveland and New York: World Publishing Co., 1950.

School Topics. [Magazine of the Public Schools of Cleveland], November 20, 1931, 1-4.

A Series of Famous Paintings Depicting the Development of Civilization in the Middle West. Cleveland: The Cleveland Trust Company, n.d.

Street, Julian. *Abroad at Home.* New York: Century Co., 1914.

Wick, Warren Corning. *My Recollections of Old Cleveland.* Cleveland: privately published, 1979.